Advance Praise for
Navigating the Out-of-Body Experience

"This book presents a fascinating review of out-of-body experiences in a detailed, yet easy-to-read style. Nicholls' valuable contribution has important implications, not only for understanding out-of-body experiences, but also by providing excellent and practical direction to help explore this phenomenon through our own personal experience."

—Dr. Jeffrey Long, *New York Times*
bestselling author of *Evidence of the Afterlife:
The Science of Near-Death Experiences*

"Though practical guides to the out-of-body experience are now plentiful, *Navigating the Out-of-Body Experience* stands out as one of the best. Wisely, Nicholls avoids unduly burdening the reader with largely useless, though entertaining, stories in favor of a careful, rational assessment of his many years of personal experience exploring OBE phenomena."

—Thomas Campbell, physicist and
author of the *My Big TOE* trilogy

NAVIGATING

THE OUT-OF-BODY

EXPERIENCE

Photo by Triin Tõniste

About the Author

Graham Nicholls (London, England) has had hundreds of out-of-body experiences and is a world-recognized expert on the subject. An experienced speaker on many areas of spirituality, art, and psychical research, he has presented his ideas at prestigious institutions such as The Science Museum of London, The London College of Spirituality, and Cambridge University. He has also been featured on the BBC and in *The Times*, *The Independent*, and the *Telegraph*, as well as in many magazines and websites.

To Write to the Author

If you wish to contact the author or would like more information about this book, please write to the author in care of Llewellyn Worldwide, and we will forward your request. Both the author and publisher appreciate hearing from you and learning of your enjoyment of this book and how it has helped you. Llewellyn Worldwide cannot guarantee that every letter written to the author can be answered, but all will be forwarded. Please write to:

Graham Nicholls
℅ Llewellyn Worldwide
2143 Wooddale Drive
Woodbury, MN 55125-2989

Please enclose a self-addressed stamped envelope for reply,
or $1.00 to cover costs. If outside the USA, enclose
an international postal reply coupon.

Many of Llewellyn's authors have websites with additional information and resources. For more information, please visit our website at: www.llewellyn.com.

GRAHAM NICHOLLS

NAVIGATING

THE OUT-OF-BODY

EXPERIENCE

RADICAL
NEW
TECHNIQUES

Llewellyn Publications
Woodbury, Minnesota

First Edition
First Printing, 2012

Book design by Bob Gaul
Cover art © Spiros Horemis/Dover Publications
Cover design by Ellen Lawson
Editing by Lee Lewis

Llewellyn Publications is a registered trademark of Llewellyn Worldwide Ltd.

Library of Congress Cataloging-in-Publication Data (Pending)
978-0-7387-2761-5

Llewellyn Worldwide Ltd. does not participate in, endorse, or have any authority or responsibility concerning private business transactions between our authors and the public.

All mail addressed to the author is forwarded, but the publisher cannot, unless specifically instructed by the author, give out an address or phone number.

Any Internet references contained in this work are current at publication time, but the publisher cannot guarantee that a specific location will continue to be maintained. Please refer to the publisher's website for links to authors' websites and other sources.

Llewellyn Publications
A Division of Llewellyn Worldwide Ltd.
2143 Wooddale Drive
Woodbury, MN 55125-2989
www.llewellyn.com

Printed in the United States of America

Contents

For Triin Tõniste.
Thank you for your light, support, and love.

Acknowledgments

I would especially like to thank my mother and father for their unending support, as well as the rest of my family and the friends who inspired and supported me during the writing process, including: Merlyn Roberts, Eucalyptus Thompson, Cecil McGrane, Matthew Dennis, Lawrence Brightman, Kadri Allikmäe, and Triin Tõniste.

I would also like to say a special thank you to Herbie Brennan for his very kind foreword to this book, and Philip Paul, Tom Campbell, Dr. Peter Fenwick, and Dr. Jeffery Long for their interviews, comments, and endorsements. I would also like to acknowledge the Society for Psychical Research, the Monroe Institute, the Institute of Noetic Sciences, and the International Association for Near Death Studies for resources and research that have helped greatly with the writing of this book. Thanks also to Alex Tsakiris for his important work moving the proponent/skeptic debate forward through the *Skeptiko* podcast and the Open Source Science project. I would also like to acknowledge Rupert Sheldrake, Brian Josephson, and Dean Radin, whose work has influenced many of the ideas that I have drawn upon.

Finally, I would like to thank Susan Mears, my agent for this book, who suggested putting the proposal forward and helped make this book a reality; Carrie Obry for championing this book at Llewellyn; Adam Schaab for taking over as editor and seeing it through to publication; and Lee Lewis, for her excellent copyediting.

Foreword

Some research polls suggest that as many as one person in every four can expect to find themselves outside their physical body and wandering the world like a ghost at some point in their life...without the inconvenience of dying in order to do so. The experience is sometimes thrilling, sometimes frightening, frequently fascinating, and almost always unexpected. For the vast majority, it is also unrepeatable.

And therein lies a major problem with what might be considered a potentially important phenomenon. Scientific investigators dislike unrepeatable evidence, which, by definition, does not lend itself to careful examination or laboratory experiment. As a result, the evidence itself is often ignored or dismissed as anecdotal. In the process, something of huge value may well be lost.

Enter Graham Nicholls. When Graham first discovered the out-of-body experience (OOBE or OBE) as a boy, he was not content to treat it as a bolt from the blue, likely never to be repeated in his lifetime. Instead, he studied, observed, and practiced until he could leave his body at will. This gave him, over the course of literally hundreds of OBEs, an opportunity to examine the phenomenon at depths unavailable to those who experience it only once, spontaneously.

In the process, he discovered there was more to the experience than met the eye. While, for many, an OBE involves no more than stepping out of the body and traveling the world in ghostly form, an OBE can also open doorways onto what appear to be different levels of reality, some of which are seemingly equivalent to the astral planes of esoteric tradition. It can also lead to changes in perception that produce a new and different understanding of the universe and can even generate the realization of unity reported by mystics down the ages. Interestingly, several of Graham's experiences were confirmed by the results of my own (unpublished) experiments in this area.

Graham's work eventually led to his first book, *Avenues of the Human Spirit*, which describes some of his experiences and presents his philosophical speculations about them. His current book goes further and in an even more exciting direction, for in it, he describes the techniques that can potentially enable you to take control of your own OBEs and, with diligent practice, develop the ability to leave your body at will.

There are a great many other books on OBEs and astral projection. (As you will soon learn, the two are not exactly the same.) A trawl of the Internet will quickly deliver scores of techniques that promise to place these fascinating experiences in your own hands. None of them—and I reluctantly place my own work in this category—can hold a candle to the book you have in your hands now. For here you have the fruits of vast personal experience, combining with penetrating intelligence, diligent observation, and a surprisingly skeptical scientific approach, to produce a work of immense value to both the psychical investigator and esoteric practitioner alike.

The key to this work lies in the final section, which describes, clearly and concisely, a multitude of methods you can use to generate an OBE. Some involve simple visualisations, like the great majority of other books on the subject, but Graham Nicholls was not content to stop there. His approaches can just as easily involve breath work, sonics, yoga, energy manipulation, even sensory deprivation techniques like Ganzfeld and the so-called "witch's cradle." His three-dimensional elaboration of the Hindu tattvas is one of the most interesting developments in the use of astral doorways since the days of the original Golden Dawn.

You may, if you wish, read the present book as no more than a fascinating account of one man's unusual adventures, but you will gain much more from it if you are prepared to embark on some adventures of your own. I urge you to experiment with Nicholls' methods for yourself, searching out those that work best for you.

Your results may well be both life-changing and, much more importantly, life-enhancing.

—J. H. (Herbie) Brennan
County Carlow, Ireland, March 2011

CELESTIAL HORIZONS:
THE ART OF LEAVING
THE BODY

I have watched the sun's rays breaking through the Earth's upper atmosphere while contemplating the swirl of oceans around the continents of the world beneath me. I have drifted through the silent vastness of space surrounded by endless stars and gaseous clouds of awe-inspiring beauty. I have seen the magnificence of the universe reflected in the structure of flowers, leaves, and stems as I looked deep into their being with my nonphysical eyes. I have experienced the profound nature of life, the interconnectedness of all that is around us. I have seen the wonders of physical and nonphysical perception. I have stood at the threshold of life and death and explored the hinterlands of consciousness. And through all of these life-changing moments, I have been aware that anyone open enough to the possibility can have similar experiences for themselves.

If we take a moment to think about it, what greater faculty could we desire than the ability to liberate ourselves from physical limitations and begin the journey of self-discovery? The out-of-body experience, or OBE as it is generally known, allows us to explore for ourselves the reality of life after physical death and perception through time, and can even afford us the freedom to travel to any place in the known universe and beyond in an instant. What's more, the OBE also begins the process of individual healing and transformation; it allows us to come into contact with our spiritual nature and find harmony and peace on a multitude of levels.

When I began my journeys beyond the body, I was a very different person. I grew up in the inner city surrounded by many social problems and few possibilities. My life was heading in a destructive direction and there seemed little possibility of anything changing. Yet, despite this environment, I had experienced some strange perceptions during my childhood and this led me to buy a book entitled *Out-of-Body Experiences: A Handbook* by Janet Lee Mitchell. I practiced every night until I experienced my first induced OBE six months later.

The result was a total change in direction in my life. I began to read about topics such as parapsychology, religion, magic, and philosophy. Soon my worldview was totally changed and, as I explored the out-of-body state, I came into contact more and more with energies and ecstatic experiences that slowly dissolved the pains of my past. Now, as I write this more than twenty years later, I still see great beauty and many possibilities awaiting me and those who would learn the art of leaving the body.

This book represents the coming together of what I have learnt over that time. This book does not require belief in supernatural powers or religious or esoteric frameworks; it makes no assumptions about the nature of the out-of-body state. It draws from all areas that I have found to be effective approaches to leaving the body, both from the last hundred and thirty years of parapsychology and my own direct experience and work with others. The result, I believe, is the most scientific approach yet in print.

My aim for this book is simple: to teach you the skills and knowledge necessary to have out-of-body experiences for yourself. Over the last twenty years, I have found that a personalized approach is the most effective way to teach someone to leave his or her body. We are all different in subtle ways: each with our own fears, needs, and emotional make-up. This book will show that with a better understanding of these needs and emotions, you will have a far greater chance of success and often in a shorter amount of time.

This tailored approach requires a process of self-enquiry that will be beneficial in all areas of your life. The first step in this process is to consider your motivations for learning to project your consciousness to another place or time. Is it simply to explore? For spiritual development? To gain greater understanding of the nature of the world around you? Or maybe to connect with someone who has passed on? Whether it is clearly one of these or a combination of factors, by understanding a little of what draws you to this exciting field, you can unravel what will motivate you most effectively toward success. The next step in the process is to understand what kind of person you are: are you emotional or analytical, an introvert or extrovert? What are the specific aspects of your identity that make you who you are, and how will they affect your goal of learning about out-of-body experiences?

Chapter 4 is an in-depth guide designed specifically to help you answer these questions and explore who you really are. Once you understand these key areas of your identity, you can go directly to the techniques in the appendix, if you like, and begin trying them out as you read through the rest of the book to deepen your understanding. These techniques have been developed and categorised so that you can select the best possible combination of options I have developed. You will have some of the most effective approaches available to help you leave your body.

These techniques are different from anything you will find in other books for several reasons, the most important of which is that they draw upon every aspect of your make-up as a person: your fears, your strengths, and also all of the sensory awareness that you use in your everyday life. This approach is designed to create a total experience, taking you more effectively into the OBE state. It is not simply a series of visualisations, as is the case with many other techniques; it is designed to use all the senses.

The design for my techniques is drawn from the science of parapsychology as well as my own research and experimentation. Parapsychology holds many clues to our psychical make-up, clues that can be put to practical use when learning to have an OBE. The history of parapsychology can be traced back to 1882 in London with the founding of the Society for Psychical Research. This enigmatic institution is still in existence to this day and has produced many excellent publications and researchers since the 1880s. Today we have far better evidence for psychic ability, or psi functioning as it is known within scientific circles. Even many skeptics admit that by the standards of any other area of science, the evidence for psi is well established. However, many remain skeptical as they claim that more research is needed. Unfortunately, those willing to ignore the nay-sayers and explore these areas are very few, as the negative impact on a scientist's career can be severe.

Yet despite the taboo against psi, there are individuals who continue to offer amazing insights into the nature of consciousness and the universe, such as consciousness researcher Michael Persinger, near-death researcher Pim Van Lommel, and "extended mind" researchers Dean Radin and Rupert Sheldrake. We will return to the findings of these individuals later, but what their work represents is a convergence of evidence in support of non-physical perception and consciousness. I draw on their research when offering ways to enhance your out-of-body experiences.

Parapsychology suggests that consciousness is "nonlocal"—in other words, that the mind may be much more like a receiver, or may exist both inside and outside of the physical brain, and so can be tuned to perceive at a distance, be that in space or time. I believe that the OBE is the most powerful way to experience and explore the outer boundaries of perception and awareness. There is no other experience open to us in which our whole sense of self is liberated from the everyday to explore, learn, and grow in such an awe-inspiring way.

What Is the OBE?

To begin, please note that I use the term *out-of-body experience* in this book to refer to a set of phenomena that appears to involve the spirit or subtle body leaving the physical body. I do not necessarily believe this is the case; terms like *leaving* and *exiting* the body are used for ease of explanation, but are not to be taken as literal facts or representative of my beliefs. As you will see, there are many exciting possibilities that could potentially explain what is taking place in an OBE, but as yet there is no clear answer to these fascinating questions.

So if I don't claim that a spirit is leaving the body during an OBE, what is an out-of-body experience? This is an extremely complex question, but it seems clear that if reality is less objective and more of a potentiality, as quantum physics seems to suggest, then the notion of bodies and even separation becomes too limited an understanding. The sensations and impressions we have during an OBE may suggest separation, but maybe it is simply a state of pure consciousness, in which we experience reality more directly. We will explore this idea more later. Others may have different opinions on this interpretation, but for the purpose of learning to have an out-of-body experience, I will define it in a more pragmatic way here:

> *An out-of-body experience (OBE) involves coherent feelings, impressions, and sensory awareness of total separation from your physical body in the form of an independent consciousness, whilst usually still being able to see and reason. The experience often involves perceiving the body from above, travel over distances, and sometimes interaction with others. The OBE can also lead to what appear to be other levels of reality. The OBE is generally described as "being as real as everyday reality."*

Many of us will have experienced something similar to this during a lucid or flying dream. However, based on my research and experiences, I would say they are very distinct states. I break it down like this:

What are the key features of a dream?

· They occur during sleep.

· We often experience rapid eye movement (REM) sleep during dreaming.

· There are no consistent defining features, such as, "All dreams begin with..."

· Dreams *generally* do not feel as real as waking reality.

What are the key features of an OBE?

· They can occur during many different states (sleep, waking, during trauma).

· Some research shows that people having OBEs are not experiencing REM sleep.

· There are many consistent features to an OBE, such as leaving the body, the silver cord, and the vibrational state.

· OBEs feel as real as waking reality.

By breaking down the key features in this way, we can see there are clear differences between OBEs and dreams. The idea that OBEs are simply a form of dream is, in my view, a misconception and one that can be unhelpful when dealing with experiences in the everyday world. When we begin to learn about other levels or planes of reality, the definitions become more subjective, but the breakdown above still serves to highlight the distinctions.

So what are the most common forms of out-of-body experience, and what is it like to have one? The most common form of OBE is the spontaneous experience. As you are reading this book, you may well be one of the 10 to 25 percent of people who have had a spontaneous out-of-body experience. They can happen in a whole range of ways, including during sleep or an illness, and sometimes even in extreme situations, such as a serious injury or cardiac arrest. However, most experiences of this type happen on what appears to be a totally average day; after you lie down to sleep, you find yourself unexpectedly floating up near the ceiling of your bedroom or in another place entirely. Some people I have spoken to over the years have had experiences of being in more than one place at the same time, and some have had OBEs induced by drugs such as ketamine or DMT. However, most of these drug-induced experiences also contain other factors on top of the generally reported out-of-body phenomena, so I tend to see them as an altered state of consciousness rather than a pure out-of-body state. During these drug experiences, consciousness may be operating in a more expansive way, but is also mixed with the everyday stuff of the mind. Of course, there are exceptions to this when dealing with mind-altering drugs, but on the whole they come into a different category.

My first encounter with being beyond my body was a spontaneous OBE. I was ten or twelve years old, and remember that on one seemingly ordinary day, I opened my eyes to find myself floating vertically around half a meter above the ground. It was very tangible; I vividly recall the grainy concrete of the playground of my childhood school. Even the cracked white paint comes to mind when I think about it, and the strange sensation of being in a familiar place yet in such an unusual way. I remember having several of these early experiences. Although it is hard to be sure whether they are true out-of-body experiences in the way I define them in this book, they did open up my interest in a way that led to me learning to induce the full out-of-body state.

It seems that most people have experiences that fall into this category at first; it is as if only part of our awareness has shifted to another vantage point, so we still retain some aspects of our sensory perception. If the spontaneous experience is the result of a more extreme situation, the exteriorisation seems to be more complete. A more complete spontaneous separation can also take place, although more rarely, when you are already asleep and wake suddenly, and attempt to get up, only to find that you are nonphysical. This can be frightening as you try to grasp what is happening, but usually does not last more than a few seconds to a few minutes.

Although these spontaneous experiences are usually brief and may only happen once or twice in a lifetime, they do still serve to inspire many of us to seek out a deeper understanding of what is going on. We may question our sanity, as researcher Robert A. Monroe did, or try to dismiss what happened as an unusual hallucination. This can seem like a reasonable thing to do, and indeed I have little doubt that some occurrences do fall within this category. But is the belief that out-of-body experiences are always simply hallucinations really a useful explanation?

If we start with the word *hallucination*, we see that it implies that what we are perceiving is false or untrue. According to the U.S. National Library of Medicine, "Hallucinations involve sensing things that aren't there while a person is awake and conscious."[1] Thus the key issue becomes: are the things that are perceived in an out-of-body experience real or illusory? This is one of the most fundamental questions related to these experiences. If what we see in an OBE is real, then the universe is even more amazing than mainstream or popular science has so far imagined. There is a divide among scientists and also among the public over this issue, so I will share some of what I have concluded on the subject.

Like all psychic abilities, OBEs are dependent upon the understanding, awareness, and state of mind of the person experiencing them. As the name implies, psychic abilities are connected to our mental faculties and therefore subject to all of our psychological strengths and limitations. This, I believe, is the clue to understanding the objective and subjective aspects of OBEs.

I have had many out-of-body experiences that could be verified afterward by physically visiting the location I had been to in the OBE or researching details from the experience. This kind of evidence is extremely important as we explore and learn more about the out-of-body state, but personal anecdotal evidence can only be part of the story, since human beings are prone to mistakes and biases.

Similarly, in research into near-death experiences (NDEs), there have been many instances of people giving details that they could not have learnt via normal means while having no heart rate or observable brain function. You may be familiar with descriptions of people who have experienced a near-fatal accident and have left their bodies and drifted into a tunnel of light, or watched the process of their resuscitation, usually from above. While not everyone experiences an OBE during an NDE, research in this field strongly suggests that OBEs are not based just upon the brain and are not simply hallucinations. There are many theories designed to explain away these life-changing events, but no one has yet offered one that explains the full complexity and detail that is communicated by those who have them. One study, by NDE researcher Dr. Penny Sartori, looks at whether people can guess what happened to them while unconscious as effectively as those who had NDEs and observed their resuscitation whilst out of the body. The results were hugely in favour of the near-death experiencers. While those guessing either had no idea or based their opinions on television or movie reconstructions, the near-death experiencers, on the other hand, were able to give accurate details of what happened to them.[2]

Another area of scientific research that supports the reality of out-of-body perception is remote viewing (RV), which is a form of psychic intelligence-gathering developed by the U.S. military during the Cold War period. In the very first book I read on OBEs, *Out-of-Body Experiences: A Handbook*, which I mentioned earlier, I learnt about work undertaken by Janet Lee Mitchell to explore evidence for perception beyond the body. She worked closely with Ingo Swann, an artist and a specialist in remote viewing. Like many of the military remote viewers, Swann was able to offer evidence to support the idea that consciousness can travel to another location and bring back factual information from that remote location. The RV program lasted for more than twenty years in the United States and has continued in other forms and in other countries. When the program ended, the research was evaluated by a statistician, Jessica Utts, and a skeptic, Ray Hyman. Even Hyman's skeptical position, in the face of the evidence in favour of remote viewing, was close to supporting the existence of psychic abilities. For example, he wrote in his report:

> *"The case for psychic functioning seems better than it ever has been. The contemporary findings along with the output of the SRI/SAIC program do seem to indicate that something beyond odd statistical hiccups is taking place. I also have to admit that I do not have a ready explanation for these observed effects."*[3]

Despite what a small group of skeptical individuals are saying, the evidence for abilities such as remote viewing and out-of-body experiences becomes stronger with each new study. When scientists are fearless and look into these little-known areas of human experience, we edge closer to an understanding of an area of life that has fascinated and inspired human beings since the earliest cultures. The scientific method offers a way of looking at the world as it really is, but we must not allow this vision of truth to be limited or hijacked by those who would tell us which avenues of inquiry are valid and which are not.

Brian Josephson, a Nobel Prize-winning physicist, has spent much of the later part of his career exploring psychic abilities and has written a theoretical model of how they might work. He has connected perception at a distance and other psi abilities with the nonlocal nature of quantum physics, especially the concept of entanglement, which states that two particles remain connected in some mysterious way despite being separated by vast distances. This contradicts much of what we once believed about the universe.

Overall, within the world of parapsychology there are various theories of how psychic abilities could work, and there is a wealth of evidence that suggests these experiences are real and objective.

When dealing with topics like the out-of-body experience, we hear many differing views on what is taking place and how it is possible. It can become very confusing to those new to the field to understand the different worldviews that writers draw upon. That is why I focus on what science is revealing. We also hear different terms when we are learning about leaving the body; this can also confuse our understanding. The most widely used of these terms include astral projection, etheric projection, and out-of-body experience. These terms are often used interchangeably, but what do they actually mean?

I'll start with probably the oldest and most widely known among these: astral projection. *Astral* comes from the Greek word *ástron*, or star, so roughly translated it means "like a star." The modern use of the term can be mainly traced to Theosophy, a worldview that seeks to blend Eastern and Western spiritual philosophies. The most notable among the Theosophist writers on the subject was A. E. Powell, who wrote books such as *The Astral Body and Other Astral Phenomena* and *The Development of Astral Powers*. Most of the books on astral projection draw upon his concepts in some form or another. He described many invisible bodies in his work, not just the astral, which he saw as being emotional in nature. The other nonphysical body he described that is important to our discussion is the etheric double, generally the body through which he believed experiences in everyday physical reality take place. He believed that the astral body, on the other hand, generally travels to the mysterious world of the astral planes.

The etheric double has its roots in a belief in the aether, dating back to the ancient Greeks. It was believed to be a kind of mystical fifth element after earth, air, fire, and water. It was sometimes seen as binding all other elements together. It is easy to see that, if there were some kind of spirit element in the universe, early writers on astral projection would suppose that this would be the substance the double was made of. The aether was also associated with air; it can be translated from the Greek to mean "pure air." As the Theosophists also drew on Eastern ideas, they soon connected the aether with *prana*, the yogic life force connected to sunlight and breathing. In fact, some even use the term *pranic body* instead of *etheric body*.

The astral and etheric bodies are the two that the vast majority of literature on astral projection focuses on, yet I have seen many invisible bodies described. Some claim this is not a literal belief in several separate and distinct bodies, but more of an understanding of different states of awareness. This way of viewing the concept seems more in tune with our modern minds, as more scientifically minded researchers recognize that there are different states or levels to the experience.

Robert A. Monroe, though not a scientist, did approach the subject in a fairly scientific way. He described what he called *locales,* which again refer essentially to different states or levels of consciousness. Locale I, for example, would relate to the etheric level, as this locale relates to experiences on the physical reality level, while Locale II would refer roughly to astral plane experiences.

It was also Monroe who popularised the term *out-of-body experience* in his 1971 book *Journeys Out of the Body.* The importance of this term lies in the fact that it does not assume the existence of a soul, spirit, etheric, or astral body. It simply notes that we experience a sense of leaving or being beyond the usual limitations of our physical body. I prefer this term over astral projection and other terms for this reason; I want to explore the experience with an enquiring mind, without a predetermined idea of what I will find or experience. When dealing with such important yet complex experiences, we owe it to future generations as well as our own integrity not to limit our worldview.

This openness when learning to have OBEs creates much more exciting possibilities. Far from setting off along a well-worn path, you will be exploring the territory of nonphysical reality for yourself. At first I drew heavily upon esoteric knowledge when I explored the out-of-body state, yet as time went by I increasingly found that my experiences did not match the worldview I had been learning about. This may have just been my experience, but the power of the exploratory approach is that you will learn for yourself and maybe even discover a level that has never been described before.

New Approaches to Having an OBE

In 1998, I began work on a series of projects that used the power of hypnosis, guided meditation, and new scientific understandings about consciousness to create special environments and structures designed to help people enter into the kind of trance states needed to have an OBE. The first of these was called an Epicene and consisted of a large, bedlike platform suspended in space by a steel frame. Once volunteers got onto the platform, they instantly experienced a feeling of floating, which many found relaxing. Once they were ready, a guided meditation began that would gently take them into a trance state. Depending on the person, some would go deeper and others would simply report a light euphoric state. Those who that went deeper sometimes reported strong emotional experiences.

At this time, I also experimented with neuro-linguistic programming (NLP), which is a form of psychological performance enhancement. I made video recordings of many people under hypnosis as I regressed them to specific points in their lives to identify their fears and limitations. This research now forms part of my OBE system, as I found that many people have a range of fears connected to what they perceive as losing control or the unknown. These fears can be transformed by understanding that we almost always remain in control in an OBE, and also that there is nothing fearful or negative about the experience. In fact, after several hundred OBEs, I have found nothing but healing and transformation within my own experiences.

A few years after my hypnosis experiments, I began researching virtual reality and was lucky enough to get the opportunity to create another large-scale immersive environment at London's Science Museum in 2004. I was using the most advanced virtual reality technology available at the time and also exploring ways that the public could interact with this technology in a way that would feel comfortable to them. I learnt a lot and developed simple forms of the technology that could be used at home.

I will explain how to make a simple immersive environment later in this book. I will also explore how churches and temples throughout history have created a form of immersion without complex technology using images, scents, and sound. This is the basis of ritual practices across the world and provides another way to induce an altered state for those who dislike the use of technology. There is even the retreat approach—going on a journey away from people and other influences for the purpose of developing your OBE skills. The key factor is immersing yourself fully in the process, whatever method you decide to use.

It was actually my total engagement with the process of learning to leave my body that led to my first induced out-of-body experience. I wasn't successful until I'd already been practising every night for six months. I have written about it in my book *Avenues of the Human Spirit*, but I will briefly recap the experience here. I had almost given up on inducing an OBE after such a long time, since I'd had little success beyond experiencing feelings of flowing energy and sometimes a sense of floating. Like most people, I would sometimes drift off into sleep or lie there for what seemed like hours in a kind of sleepy trance state. Yet somehow all of this had been building steadily over the months of practice; I was beginning to understand my own psychological landscape in ways I didn't even realise at the time.

On the night I finally succeeded, I remember lying there when a jolt of energy shot through my body, something akin to a large electrical shock. It wasn't painful, but it was very close to that level of intensity. As I regained awareness of my surroundings, I realised I was hovering or floating around a meter above my physical body, fixed in a horizontal position while unable to move forward and backward or up and down. I could only rotate as if a pole extended the length of my body. I remember looking at the window and, as I did, I was aware of vibrant energy pulsing and flowing all around. This energy seemed to colour my bedroom with a blue, hazy light.

My physical body below hardly seemed like me; if I could not have made out my features and known where I was, I may not have recognized it. It seemed stony, grayed-out, and motionless. It was a very strange sight, yet it didn't seem important or frightening, since I felt like I was the shimmering, floating form, not the still, silent body below me.

I'm not sure how long it lasted, as this is not noted in my diary, but it was a fairly short experience. Yet after this small success, my confidence returned and I found a new drive to experience more. Things were much easier after this, too. I experienced energy pulses and flowing waves even before I left my body, and I learnt that this signaled that I could bring on an experience.

Many people experience similar waves of energy, or vibrations as some authors have described them. I feel a lightening of my body and a sense of energy flowing in a wavelike, rhythmic movement. If I focus on this sense and allow myself to go with it, I often find that an OBE will follow. I first experienced this state early on in my six-month learning period, but I tended to focus on the idea of "projection." This is an example of how a preconception can hinder you. I have found it far better to turn inward or simply surrender to the waves rather than try to use conscious will.

Different people experience the sensation of leaving the body in different ways. Some float out of their bodies, as in the case of Sylvan Muldoon, coauthor of the classic book on the subject, *The Projection of the Astral Body;* others almost roll out of their bodies. I generally "phase" to another location or gently float upward. Early on, I was far more likely to remain in my immediate physical surroundings. But now when I leave my body, I often seem to bypass the exiting part of the experience and find myself at a distant location without even the sense of traveling there. This seems to indicate a kind of traveling consciousness, as opposed to the idea that an etheric body leaves and travels to another location. In fact, many of my experiences seem to resemble a sense of moving as a conscious framework, a kind of traveling awareness rather than a body of any sort.

Sometimes, however, I do experience a body that usually seems to glow and to be made of some kind of translucent energy. This resembles classical descriptions from the literature of astral projection. For example, a very recent experience entailed floating out of my body and drifting to one of the large windows in my bedroom. As I came to the window ledge, I put my hands out in front of me, much as I would if I was stopping myself physically. I felt a slight resistance—although more in expectation of resistance, I would say—as my hands passed through the glass and frame and I drifted out above the street. I turned, hanging in the air and looking at the long, empty street. I was aware of my subtle body floating, the sensation much like treading water, but without the need to move, just a feeling that I was supported by something. My limbs and torso seemed normal, a double of my physical body but also surrounded by and radiating a misty haze of colour, mainly blue, though sometimes other shades would arise and flow through my form, too.

I have also experienced standing on the street, watching people passing by and taking in what is happening around me. In a few of these experiences, I have not felt myself travel nor even wanted to move; I have simply remained stationary and observed the events unfolding. In yet another experience, I vividly felt the sensation of my body as I circled a large mountain and slowly ascended to the level of the peak. All around the beauty of the snow and ice sparkled in the dawn light. In the distance, I could see valleys and possibly the signs of small villages or communities.

Through my OBEs, I have regained a sense of wonder, as I have never known what I might see or experience. And even more than that, it is the avenues that these experiences lead you down in everyday life that make them so powerful and life-affirming. I have experienced all the amazing possibilities that I read about as a teenager, which fascinated me enough to learn to project my consciousness. Yet I have never experienced one of the classic elements of an OBE, the silver cord—like a kind of umbilical cord attaching us to our physical bodies.

The silver cord has a long history dating back many centuries. Do not be surprised if you do experience one, or if you don't; it seems to be related to the individual and is not important to the quality of your experiences. As I will remind you throughout this book, the more you are open to allowing the experience to take its own form, the better. The more you try to define it or build up expectations, the more you limit yourself in a way that will probably be unhelpful. The more we allow ourselves freedom and move away from influences that undermine the integrity of our state of mind, the more new experiences can take shape.

Learning to experience something new can be as much about changing and moving away from old habits as learning new concepts and practices. It takes a revolution of our inner spirit to bring the extraordinary fully into our lives. This change also requires us to be radically honest about ourselves. Be prepared to be as truthful as possible when thinking about your strengths and weaknesses, since by doing this you will reach your goals more effectively.

When I began my quest to have controlled out-of-body experiences, the one thing that more than anything else allowed me to succeed was a drive and passion for learning and experiencing. I was determined not to fail and was willing from the start to put my whole focus into what I was doing. As we walk down one avenue in life, we walk away from another; we must have the courage to grow and transform in ways we never imagined. The reward is a life full of exploration, experience, and wonder.

2

SCIENCE AND
THE OUT-OF-BODY
EXPERIENCE

S cience, like spiritual disciplines, helps us to look deeply at the age-old
questions of human existence. The scientific approach is focused on
truth in the sense that it seeks to uncover the way things really are. Esoteric
philosophies, on the other hand, while offering insight and creative ways
of looking at the nature of reality, do not have this objective understanding drawn from precise observation. However, one of the practices of many
esoteric systems, meditation, does have much in common with science. I
like the analogy of a still mind: by reaching a state in which all thoughts

and emotional imbalances are stilled, we can see with truth and clarity. This is actually a trait that meditation and science share—a clear perception of the way things are. They differ in that meditation focuses on the self and the limitations of the ego, while science focuses on that which is tangible and measurable. As I mention in my first book, many great scientists throughout history have worked in an almost meditative state. Think of Newton or Einstein's ability to visualize the laws of the universe. Through reason and logic, they were able to comprehend nature and the forces at play in a vast and impersonal cosmos.

In this chapter, I want to introduce you to the fascinating world of parapsychology and show how this field of research can improve your understanding of the mechanics of out-of-body experiences. Most books on the subject offer personal experiences or traditional methods, both of which have merit in understanding the OBE, but science is based upon a more expansive, continually evolving understanding. If we are able to understand what is happening inside the brain when someone is perceiving information without the use of the five physical senses, we might be able to help someone else learn the same skill by generating the same state in their brain. This can be achieved through neuro-feedback, for example, and is just one example of how advances in science can help us reach levels of awareness that were not possible generations ago. As you read this chapter, keep in mind that all of the areas I mention give clues to the true nature of the out-of-body state, and techniques from those areas can often be directly applied to help us leave the body. To begin, we need to make sure that we are clear on the definition of science.

So What Is Science?

Let me start by saying what science is not. Science is not a body of dogma, nor an institution that holds all available knowledge about the world. Science is, in fact, simply a method of inquiry, combined with the analysis and comprehension of the results of that method. Genuine science is a life-changing way of understanding ourselves and our place in the world. Here is a formal definition I put together:

> *Science is a method of acquiring knowledge, usually about the natural world or the universe, by applying the principles of the scientific method, which include making precise observations, proposing hypotheses to explain those observations, and testing those hypotheses in a controlled manner, such as through double- or triple-blind experiments. The results of these experiments are usually published in a peer-reviewed journal within the relevant field for critique, exchange, and replication of the findings by others.*

This definition references the *scientific method*, which can be the source of some confusion. Generally, when we hear about science in the media and in other sources, it is referred to as if it is simply a body of information and facts about the world. What would be more accurate is to say that by using the methods of science, we gain a clearer understanding of the world, which other scientists can observe and agree upon.

What is the scientific method?

The scientific method can be broken down into five key points:

1. Observe a phenomenon that has no good explanation.

2. Formulate a hypothesis based upon observation of this phenomenon.

3. Design an experiment to test the hypothesis.

4. Perform the experiment.

5. Accept, reject, or modify the hypothesis based upon the results obtained.

The out-of-body experience clearly falls into the area of "phenomenon with no good explanation," so in our quest to better understand it, we need to observe what is actually taking place in an OBE and develop a hypothesis based upon what we find. In my opinion, two key elements need to be better understood if we are to come up with an accurate and workable understanding of what an OBE is. First is the objective evidence in favour of remote-viewing experiments and other studies of nonlocal perception. Second is the extremely complex area of the near-death experience (NDE). Thus the question becomes whether remote perception is possible, plus whether it is possible without an active, "living" brain.

Few scientists have applied the scientific method to the out-of-body experience, perhaps because some theories—such as a lack of oxygen to the brain contributing to an OBE—can be difficult to test scientifically. Also hindering objective investigation is a misguided belief by some skeptics that they are attacking superstition and pseudoscience.

The first rule of the scientific method (observe a phenomenon that has no good explanation) must be followed as objectively as possible to avoid any sort of bias. A religious believer, for example, who goes into an experiment with a predefined belief about the world is breaking this rule if he or she does not observe the nature of the phenomenon *as it is*. He or she may also break the fifth rule (accept, reject, or modify the hypothesis based upon the results obtained) if the findings do not match his preconceptions. The skeptic who goes into an experiment with a notion that the phenomenon is false is also breaking scientific protocol.

Back in 1990, when I induced my first out-of-body experience, the most influential book I read on the subject was by a parapsychologist, Janet Lee Mitchell. In it, she described what people actually experience when out of the body *based on scientific observation*. Her description was stripped of all religious or esoteric language; instead, it was clear, insightful, and factual. Similarly, it was obvious to me that this book should be based upon what parapsychology has discovered over the last 130 years. Science has identified many factors—ranging from the impact of sunspot activity to the physical and emotional state of the subject—that indicate likely success in out-of-body and psi experiences, whether the scientist involved believes the experiences to be objectively real, or not.

As a student of OBEs, you will find it extremely helpful to use a scientific viewpoint when learning. As you have your first experiences, you may find that they have certain characteristics that may well be unique to you. The more careful you are in recording them, the better your understanding will become, and you will be able to fine-tune your approach.

The Extended Mind Theory

In Chapter 1, I briefly mentioned a group of innovative scientists exploring the nature of consciousness and what they refer to as the "extended mind"—the idea that mind (consciousness) and brain are not identical, but may exist in relationship to each other, rather than mind simply being the result of brain function and nothing more. One of the main scientists in this group is Dr. Rupert Sheldrake, a biologist and psi researcher based in London. He is the author of more than eighty scientific papers and ten books. A former Research Fellow of the Royal Society, he studied natural sciences at Cambridge University, where he was a Scholar of Clare College. I worked with him in 2009 on a joint project looking at telephone telepathy and continue to take an active interest in his research.

As part of Sheldrake's research into plants, he began to question the generally accepted idea that you could discover everything about a plant by cutting it into smaller and smaller parts and looking at these parts in isolation. Instead, he thought that looking at the function of a life form as a whole would reveal more about it and how its complexity and form arises. This later led to his theory of "morphic fields," or the idea that the structure and final form of a plant or animal could not be fully explained by genes or reductionism, and that a field may exist around all living things that organises their final complexity. He soon saw that these fields could exist in other forms beyond the plant and animal kingdoms and began to consider the idea that even social groups could function in this collective way.

If these fields exist, as Sheldrake believes, this could account for the idea that information is nonlocal; in other words, that thoughts and memories—in fact, all the things that we associate with the mind—could be extended outside of our brains within these morphic fields. He has put the case for the extended mind thus: "The mind may be extended not only in space but also in time. We may all draw upon a collective memory, similar to the collective unconscious postulated by C.G. Jung."[1]

Is there any scientific basis for the idea of the collective unconscious? Is the extended mind a supernatural or a natural phenomenon? It is clear that we do not have a conclusive answer to these questions yet, but the work of many scientists shows that the extended mind is a real possibility.

The extended mind is not the same as the out-of-body state—or is it? I believe that this depends upon your perspective of what an OBE is and where it takes place. When in the out-of-body state, I experience the world around me from the vantage point of a kind of traveling awareness, sometimes with a body, sometimes without. What this suggests to me is that the experience takes on the form that my consciousness or awareness is aligned to at that particular time. Sheldrake posits that there are fields that contain information about a plant or animal that can develop and change as new information comes into that field: "Morphic fields organize atoms, molecules, crystals, organelles, cells, tissues, organs, organisms, societies, ecosystems, planetary systems, solar systems, galaxies. In other words, they organize systems at all levels of complexity."[2]

Could then the OBE be a kind of field of consciousness that, depending upon the habits and behaviours of the person involved, changes and develops over time? If there is a "second body," then could it too be a form built up by the behaviour and nature of the person involved? It is an interesting possibility and, in fact, one that seems to bring together the concept of a second or subtle body with the concept of an extended awareness of consciousness. It shows that these two ideas need not be totally separate: that in fact the second body and our extended consciousness may be one and the same.

The morphic field theory, which sees mind as extended through these frameworks of information, is one explanation for the out-of-body experience. Another explanation is that our consciousness can appear to us to be in another location because it is entangled on a quantum level of our physical universe.

The Quantum Entanglement Theory

The out-of-body experience is often placed into the domain of the supernatural, especially by those skeptical of the objective nature of such experiences. The debate between skeptics and proponents often revolves around the idea, on one side, that there is nothing but a brain producing an illusory framework we call consciousness, and on the other extreme, that there is a spirit or soul that survives bodily death and has little to do with natural laws. My position does not include the supernatural; I see the OBE as a natural phenomenon possibly resulting from an extended form of consciousness or mind. This is also the approach that most scientifically based proponents take.

The still-evolving field of quantum physics suggests an alternate possibility. The clearest theory put forward thus far to show that psychic abilities could be based in objective reality was outlined by Brian Josephson, a British physicist who won the Nobel Prize in 1973. He studied at Cambridge University and went on to head their Mind-Matter Unification project. He draws upon Bell's Theorem, an important aspect of quantum physics, to suggest that the interconnected nature of reality could extend to biological organisms such as human beings. This essentially means that the processes of thought and memory could be extended across any distance, regardless of space and time, as quantum entanglement has been shown not to be bound by limitations such as the speed of light.

While the idea of an extended mind has not been proven, it is becoming a solid possibility in light of recent findings, including research by Rita Pizzi, from The State University of Milan, that appears to demonstrate nonlocality in human brain cells.[3] This challenges many of the arguments against nonlocality as a workable theory of psychic abilities, such as the longstanding belief that entanglement does not "scale up" to the level of cells and therefore brains.

Another researcher who seems to have demonstrated entanglement between minds directly is Michael Persinger, a professor and cognitive neuroscience researcher at Laurentian University in Ontario, Canada. He is best known for his work with the Koren helmet, or as it is more popularly known, the "God helmet." The device uses "transcranial magnetic stimulation" and appears to stimulate the temporal lobes of the brain in such a way as to cause hallucinations or sensations much like those described in meditation or a numinous experience. But his work does not end with the assumption that because he can stimulate hallucinations, there is little else to explore. Instead, he looked at the idea that telepathy and other psi phenomena could be enhanced in a similar way. In a conversation with Alex Tsakiris of the *Skeptiko* podcast, Persinger said, "What we have found is that if you place two different people at a distance and put a circular magnetic field around both, and you make sure they are connected to the same computer so they get the same stimulation, then if you flash a light in one person's eye, the person in the other room receiving just the magnetic field will show changes in their brain as if they saw the flash of light. We think that's tremendous because it may be the first macro demonstration of a quantum connection, or so-called quantum entanglement. If true, then there's another way of potential communication that may have physical applications, for example, in space travel."[4]

Ironically, despite Persinger offering some thought-provoking research into telepathy, his work with magnetic fields and the brain is often used by skeptics to dismiss experiences such as OBEs. Such claims will be discussed later, but Persinger does not see the fact that he can induce experiences of a mystical type in his subjects as disproving psi. On the contrary, his work suggests he may be able to enhance and even improve psi abilities in the future.

Contributing Factors in Psi Success

Emotions and memory

Rupert Sheldrake and Dean Radin have shown that emotional bonds and emotion in general allow for greater connection in telepathy trials.

Ganzfeld telepathy experiments in particular have consistently shown that interconnections between people can be demonstrated empirically. The Ganzfeld process is a form of mild sensory deprivation that was introduced into psychology in the 1930s, and was later used by parapsychologists studying telepathy. It will be explored on a practical level later in this book. According to Dean Radin, a senior scientist at the Institute of Noetic Sciences in California and author of two in-depth books looking at the field of parapsychology, the statistical odds against chance in favour of telepathy in the Ganzfeld experiments stands at 29 quintillion to 1.[5] Radin has also shown that advanced meditators have greater ability to control their psychic functions.

For our purposes, it may be helpful to familiarise yourself with the emotional traits that benefit psychic abilities. Empathy seems useful in working with telepathy, and I have also found that those who develop their artistic skills in a natural way can improve their psychic abilities. Michael Persinger has shown that people with high temporal lobe sensitivity can more easily have mystical experiences.[6]

Memory techniques provide a useful way of working on your visualisation skills that can also be easily tested. This is because memory recall has much in common with psychic perception. For example, when teaching some of these techniques, I asked a student to describe the interior of a building that we both knew well. She was able to recall major elements about the space, such as the layout of the building and large obvious structures, but when I asked her about the design of the walls and details such as the colour of the chairs, she was unable to describe them. I have found this is very similar to what we experience in our OBEs. In one of my own experiences, I found myself looking at a large building, and later I was able to describe its unusual structural elements, in this case, Egyptian-influenced designs. However, I was unable to describe the colour of the building or specifics about the structures. Memory in this sense may be linked to our ability to observe; the more we develop our observation skills, the more our OBE perceptions improve. Let's explore two methods for working with memory.

The link method

Create a visual image of the concept or item you are trying to remember, and link it to a physical attribute. Some people imagine a scene and then add the item to the scene. With practice, the scene or place you use becomes familiar and the process gets easier. This is especially useful in learning to have OBEs, since it creates a strong awareness of space and the location of the object within space.

The story method

Instead of imagining a scene or a place, you create a story featuring the elements you want to remember. Suppose you want to remember the colours red, green, blue, and yellow and the numbers four, eight, and ten. You could create a story in which you and four friends get into a red car and drive to a green open space like a park. The park is surrounded by eight trees, under which you laid out a blue blanket and ten yellow cups.

Planetary influences

In the mid-1980s, Michael Persinger, studying telepathy, and Marcia Adams, studying remote viewing, both found a relationship between success in their experiments and days when the magnetic field from the sun was quiet.[7] Similarly, Charles Tart explained in a paper on the subject that the sun's magnetic field has several tangible effects on the Earth, including the aurora borealis.[8] However, these effects were weak and, as with many psi-related phenomena, it is extremely hard to show a solid connection.

Krippner et al. found evidence that the moon had an even more powerful effect: "We found that psi seemed to operate better on nights of the full moon."[9] This idea has been popular for centuries, but when I read the article, I was skeptical about whether it was anything more than coincidence. To test the concept, I went back through my diary entries from many years of my OBEs, noting down significant events. The result was that some 75 percent of my notable experiences took place within five days before a full moon. This was interesting, as I had made the diary entries years before without any reference to the moon, and I also made the list of major experiences before I used a computer program to find the moon phase at the time. Virtually none of my experiences were actually on the full moon.

In a practical sense, I recommend that you experiment during the run-up to the full moon. You may find that the process of inducing the vibrational state or having a full out-of-body experience is easier at these times.

It may simply be that the moon is suggestive to us of something mysterious and beyond the normal realm of understanding, and this appeals to us on the unconscious level. The unconscious mind, and our beliefs and motivations, have a huge impact on success in virtually all human endeavors, as we will explore next.

The unconscious mind

On a day-to-day level, we are only ever aware of a small portion of the vast store of memories, motivations, and beliefs that exist beneath our awareness in what is known as the unconscious or subconscious mind. Much of our success in attempting to leave the body seems grounded in our ability to be in tune with this hidden aspect of ourselves. If the conscious and unconscious minds are in conflict in some way, the process becomes harder.

Dreams are the main experience people think of when they imagine ideas bubbling up from the unconscious level. These sometimes strange nighttime perceptions offer us clues about our emotional state, our daily lives, and our desires. But most of us are not fully aware of our dreams, because they are largely ignored as we go about the more pressing aspects of our daily lives. The first step, therefore, in becoming more attuned to psychic development is to give attention to our unconscious world in the form of recording our dreams. This is not simply a process of waking up and noting down what you were dreaming about, but also becoming aware of what you felt and saw, as well as the symbolic meaning behind the dream. The best way to do this is to take a few minutes and reconnect to the dream experience as soon as you wake. Let yourself drift back to the edge of the dream state. Try to drift as far back in this perception as you can without falling asleep again. I call this reconnecting, and with practice you can reach a point where you can sense how the dream arose. The point at which a dream arises marks the point between a purely unconscious state and a semiconscious state such as a dream. Become aware of this point of awareness—how does it feel? What do you sense? Note all of this in your journal.

The next step is to use this awareness to become conscious as the dream arises. This is called *lucid dreaming*, which means to have greater awareness and control during the dream state. It is essentially a state in which your conscious mind has reconnected with your unconscious landscape. From this point on, you can explore and begin to see how your consciousness is capable of much more than we imagine, both in and outside of our body awareness. A voice recording device such as a dictaphone is a useful tool when learning to have lucid dreams, since recording yourself is a great way to communicate with your unconscious. Make a recording of a positive affirmation, for example, "I wish to experience being beyond my body with total freedom, joy, and awareness tonight." This can be played back, over and over, while you go to sleep or shortly before you go to sleep. You can also use the recorder to record details of your dreams or OBEs when you wake the next morning. Our culture is dominated by visual messages, so a visual format can be used in a similar way as audio recordings, to suggest to your unconscious mind what you want to achieve. Footage of flying, views of landscapes from above, and images of energy and light all suggest the key elements of an OBE. Focusing on these kinds of images right before bedtime may help you edge closer to your goals.

How Remote Viewing and Near-Death Experiences Relate to OBEs

It seems to me that the line between remote viewing, near-death experiences, and out-of-body experiences is very thin. The distinction may even be a matter of degree; in other words, the same mental state may exist in each experience, but with varying levels of depth. Remote viewing, in this sense, is like a mild form of OBE—a state in which perception at a distance is possible, but awareness at the location of the physical body also exists. In an out-of-body experience, by usual definitions, perception is fully separate from the physical body. This is directly related to the concept of nonlocal consciousness.

Remote viewing

Remote viewing (RV), as discussed briefly in Chapter 1, was developed as a system of controlled clairvoyance—the ability to perceive information at a distance through a faculty other than the usual physical senses—and was an attempt to utilise psychic abilities for the purpose of intelligence gathering. The term *remote viewing* was coined on December 8, 1971, by Ingo Swann, Dr. Janet Mitchell, Dr. Karlis Osis, and Dr. Gertrude Schmeidler at the American Society for Psychical Research (ASPR) in New York City.[10] Over the twenty years that Project Stargate, as it was later known, was in existence, some compelling evidence was amassed for the ability to move one's consciousness to various locations in space and/or time. It is excellent practice to use the RV approach when exercising our psychic faculties. Here is a simple exercise.

Exercise: Remote viewing

Start by finding a comfortable seat at a desk or table with plenty of paper and a pen. Have a friend preselect a "target" for you and seal an image of that target in an opaque envelope.

- Step 1: Sit down and go through a relaxation process (perhaps the Deep Breathing Technique; see page 180). Joseph McMoneagle, one of the original U.S. military remote viewers, calls this period the "cool-down"—a time to clear the mind of random thoughts. You want to reach a point at which your mind is like a blank canvas ready to receive impressions.

- Step 2: Close your eyes tightly, or use an eye-mask so that you are looking into pure blackness. Impressions will begin to arise, probably in the form of images initially. These first images should feel different from your day-to-day thoughts and your imagination, as if they are arising from some external source. They will also seem more detailed than imagination; they may even be extremely vivid, possibly more so than your physical sight. Draw these initial impressions. Try not to interpret what you are seeing, especially in terms of scale.

· Step 3: Now try to bring in any other sensory impressions: are you aware of the temperature, or maybe the wind? What about smells, or noise? Try to get a clear sense of the type of location you are in. Simply write down keywords on the paper, such as sandy, dry, hot, or whatever the impressions may be.

· Step 4: Next, try to make a deeper connection with the target. How do you feel? Do you have a good feeling here, or a sense that this is the site of something more emotionally complex? Again, write down your impressions in keywords or short sentences.

· Step 5: Try to establish a connection with the target from a different perspective, maybe viewing it from above or moving to another part of the target.

· Step 6: Cross-reference any new information with your original information. How was this new perspective different? What new impressions arose?

· Step 7: To conclude, open the target envelope and assess how well you did. Don't be put off if you get "misses"; the best remote viewers in the world do. It is more important to learn how to distinguish the "misses" from the "hits." You may get a stronger sense that you are "on target" in some trials than in others. This will start to train you to recognize when you are on the right track.

Near-death experiences (NDEs)

The work of Pim Van Lommel, a Dutch cardiologist and researcher who conducted the largest study to date of near-death experiences, draws upon the idea that our consciousness may be nonlocal in nature. He believes that there is objective, repeatable evidence for this claim, and that quantum entanglement may lie at the root of NDEs and the out-of-body perception that is usually a part of them.

Van Lommel puts forward the idea that our consciousness may be the result of various nonlocal interactions, rather than simply being a function of the brain. He uses the analogy of a television: "Could our brain be compared to the TV set, which receives electromagnetic waves and transforms them into image and sound, as well as to the TV camera, which transforms image and sound into electromagnetic waves? This electromagnetic radiation holds the essence of all information, but is only perceivable by our senses through suitable instruments like the camera and TV set."[11]

If this is the case, much of what makes up our consciousness would exist outside of our brain. Van Lommel states that it is an "almost unavoidable conclusion that at the time of physical death, consciousness will continue to be experienced in another dimension, in an invisible and immaterial world, the phase-space, in which all past, present, and future is enclosed."[12] Dr. Penny Sartori, who is known for conducting the UK's first and largest long-term clinical study of NDEs, has shown that those who have had NDEs can sometimes perceive highly accurate, verifiable facts about their resuscitation that they could not have known otherwise. This is powerful evidence in favour of the NDE being at least partly objective, since patients were able to observe events from an out-of-body vantage point. Sartori went on to say in an interview with the BBC, "All the current skeptical arguments against near-death experiences were not supported by the research."[13] She also states, "Current science says [consciousness] is a by-product of the brain. But it may be that consciousness is around us and the brain might be a mediator, an antenna, instead of controlling consciousness." This echoes the conclusions of Pim Van Lommel, Peter Fenwick, and Rupert Sheldrake, among others.

The secrets of science reveal that we are intimately linked to the world and the universe around us, and that our inner awareness can experience the world without the need for a body or our physical senses. As our understanding grows, I suspect this intimate connection, this oneness, will become more apparent, and the line between us and the cosmos will become arbitrary.

3

SKEPTICS AND THE OUT-OF-BODY EXPERIENCE

S ome of you reading this book may be unsure about the objective reality of out-of-body experiences. Maybe you are reading it out of a desire to decide for yourself whether or not the experience is real. This is a very understandable and healthy position to take. If we don't learn to have an inquiring, yet skeptical, way of looking at things, we will simply be lost in the cultural baggage of our upbringing, or worse, be drawn along by the interests of mass media. A skeptical inquiring mind is especially important when we begin to explore areas like the OBE. We are dealing with an area that is full of beliefs and claims that lie outside of our reasonable understanding, so without skepticism we are literally lost.

Webster's defines skepticism as "an attitude of doubt or a disposition to incredulity, either in general or toward a particular object; the doctrine that true knowledge or knowledge in a particular area is uncertain."[1] In other words, genuine skepticism is simply about looking in an objective way at our own beliefs, as well as the claims that people make. It is about learning rather than believing. If we don't investigate psychological or mundane explanations for what we experience in the world, we have little chance of ever understanding what is happening to us. It was, in fact, this question—what is happening to me?—that first led me to explore science and skepticism. However, it soon became obvious to me that what is generally referred to as "skepticism" is often a movement of activists with an agenda that can result in a limiting of scientific inquiry.

In this chapter, I will explore the differences between healthy, inquiring skepticism and the popular movement. I will keep this investigation focused on those who deal with the out-of-body experience as we explore what they say and whether they and their views hold up in any real sense. As many writers have noted, the best evidence for the OBE will no doubt come from your own exploration, yet I also believe that we need the tools to assess those experiences, and that's exactly what a scientific and skeptical understanding can help us do.

You may have read reports in the press over the last few years claiming that out-of-body experiences are illusory, and that they can be easily produced via brain stimulation. In fact, despite these reports in popular press such as *Time* magazine, *New Scientist*, the *New York Times*, and others, there has never been a convincing replication of an OBE in the laboratory. Even if there had been, I would wonder if this would mean as much to our understanding of the subject as has been claimed. A hallucinatory experience does not, logically speaking, disprove the existence of the object of the hallucination. For example, if I hallucinate that a car just drove by my upstairs window, it does not follow that cars do not exist! Unfortunately, popular or media skepticism relies heavily on this logical fallacy. Skeptics will demonstrate that a similar experience or event can be created by trickery or psychological means as a tool to convince uninformed members of the public that all psychic phenomena must therefore be false. This blind spot in their reasoning shows that we are not simply dealing with a different take on the evidence, which is valid and acceptable, but instead a clear and obvious bias. While I believe that media skepticism has a role to play when dealing with charlatans such as fake mediums and others, it can hinder our understanding if explanations are offered for phenomena prematurely.

The Skeptical Community

The popular skeptical community is not simply a grouping of individuals supporting scientific understanding; it is an active, organised network engaged in activism with the aim of silencing or attacking those they deem to be on the side of superstition and ignorance while also rejecting scientific investigation of psychical phenomena. The mantra of this movement is "extraordinary claims require extraordinary evidence," usually credited to Carl Sagan.[2]

Yet where does this quote originate and what does it really mean? Sagan actually borrowed this phrase from Marcello Truzzi, a sociologist and prominent skeptic who had a far more careful understanding of genuine skepticism. His version reads, "When such claims are extraordinary, that is, revolutionary in their implications for established scientific generalizations already accumulated and verified, we must demand extraordinary proof."[3] Ironically, Truzzi turned against many of the media skeptics and came to view them as "pseudoskeptics," to use his term. He believed that those who dispute the reality of fields such as out-of-body experiences or psychic abilities are also making a claim and must therefore, by scientific standards, also prove it: "If a critic asserts that there is evidence for disproof, that he has a negative hypothesis—saying, for instance, that a seeming psi result was actually due to an artifact—he is making a claim and therefore also has to bear a burden of proof."[4]

This is an important point, as popular skepticism often operates by hiding behind the "burden of proof," which is always on the claimant in science. Truzzi shows here that this burden is also on those who make negative claims. He points out that reliance on an "artifact" or unknown factor, as a way of dismissing evidence, is not valid and is actually unscientific.

Next we'll look at three key individuals promoting skeptical arguments against the objectivity of out-of-body experiences.

Susan Blackmore

The most well-known skeptic of out-of-body experiences may be Susan Blackmore, a British writer and lecturer who studied psychology and physiology at Oxford University and gained a Ph.D. in parapsychology from the University of Surrey. She now spends most of her time writing and speaking on subjects related to consciousness, but for many years was prominent, especially on British television, offering possible explanations for various psychic phenomena.

Blackmore's interest in parapsychology began as a university student when she had a cannabis-induced episode that included several elements in common with out-of-body and near-death experiences. In her 1996 book, *In Search of the Light*, she describes experiencing a whole range of complex phenomena, such as a dark tunnel and flying over vast distances. However, there were many questionable elements to the experience. For example, she states that she was able to communicate with others present in the room at the time. This is very suggestive to me that her experience was more of a hallucination than a full OBE. I find this unsurprising since it was the result of both drug use and an evening of highly suggestive paranormal discussion.

Regardless of the subjectivity of Blackmore's experience, it is clear it had a profound impact on her and led to a desire to explore, and even prove, the validity of psychic phenomena. She began a series of experiments in areas such as telepathy over an approximately two-year period. Based on her consistent failure in these experiments, she came to the conclusion that out-of-body experiences, and psi abilities in general, were false.

I do believe that this rejection of psi was a genuine shift in her belief system, as she was unable to obtain the positive results in her psychic experiments that others were getting. However, some such as Chris Carter,[5] an expert on the skeptical community, believe it was her own failings as a scientist that resulted in a misguided conclusion. In fact, she admits that her experiments were poorly designed. In a reply to Rick Berger's critical examination of her experiments, she said, "I am glad to be able to agree with his final conclusion— 'that drawing any conclusion, positive or negative, about the reality of psi that is based on the Blackmore psi experiments must be considered unwarranted.'"[6]

So what are we to make of Blackmore's position? She states on the one hand that it was her investigation of psychic phenomena that convinced her these areas are not real, but on the other hand, when challenged she admits that her own work cannot be the basis of any conclusions.

We are forced to be very careful when taking her opinions as anything other than personal. This is highlighted by her lack of awareness of much of the current (and earlier) research. In a lecture by her that I attended in 2008, she stated that she had never read the major U.S. military remote viewing research, commonly known as the Stargate material, when it was made available. She stated that she was so disillusioned with parapsychology at that point, she decided to not read it.[7] Further, in an interview with Alex Tsakiris in 2010, she admitted that her ideas were now fifteen years out of date with regard to near-death experience research.[8] This would not be an issue since she has left the field, but her ideas are still widely referenced.

Blackmore also wrote a book on OBEs, *Beyond the Body* (1983), in which she explored the then-current evidence. Although very in-depth in many ways (and I do agree with some of her conclusions), it did leave out much of the evidence in favour of nonlocal consciousness. It also drew conclusions based on a lack of evidence, as unfortunately there has been very little research devoted specifically to out-of-body experiences. So at best we can say that her book went some way to dispel some myths about the nature of OBEs, but was ultimately limited by a lack of specific research to draw upon.

Blackmore's main theory to explain the out-of-body experience is that it is a form of sleep paralysis and therefore illusory. Although I must state I have never personally experienced sleep paralysis or paralysis as part of the process of having an OBE, it seems that a very few people do experience this, as Blackmore points out in her paper on the subject: "In surveys, Green found that 5 percent of OBErs reported paralysis at some stage, and Poynton found 7 percent."[9] This seems to me a very low percentage on which to base a theory.

Blackmore further describes sensations, such as buzzing, humming, and vibrations. These are very vague terms, and of course it is common that such descriptions are vague, but that leads me to conclude we can draw very little from them. Blackmore states, "These results suggest that there is considerable overlap between the two experiences of OBEs and sleep paralysis."[10] Yet, although there is "overlap," it is a long way from offering an explanation or drawing the conclusion that these experiences are in the brain alone, and that there is no objective factor. To do that, the findings of NDE researchers and the objective evidence from other areas of psi research would need to be addressed. I also feel that a more precise exploration of the descriptions of both out-of-body experiencers and those undergoing sleep paralysis would be needed to really determine whether or not there is a relationship between the two.

So what can we take away from Blackmore's work? While I think that her opinions are as honest as any individual's can be, and her willingness to sometimes admit when she is wrong is admirable, there are two main problems for me with her position and conclusions. First, her research was discredited by her own admission and, second, she is simply one individual. There are many researchers who have gained consistent, significant, and positive results in psychic experiments and continue to do so. That is an example of why science doesn't base its conclusions on one person's research. If it did, a vocal individual like Blackmore might be enough to convince many that something untrue was in fact true. I feel this may be exactly what has happened within the skeptical community with Blackmore; we have someone who admits her work was flawed and her knowledge outdated, yet she is still quoted as a leading expert in areas such as the near-death experience, despite the fact that she gave up parapsychology some fifteen years ago.

Olaf Blanke

Olaf Blanke is a Swiss medical doctor with a Ph.D. in neurophysiology, the study of the function of the nervous system. This led him to the study of self consciousness, or how our understanding and awareness of ourselves is constructed. This includes how we are conscious of the position and activities of the body in space. For example, I know where my hands are as I write these words, I'm aware of the feeling of them typing, and my visual sense matches what I feel. In Blanke's research, the aim is to understand how all of this sensory information is put together. This led to experiments that attempt to alter our sensory awareness, essentially by tricking the mind through technology such as virtual reality or stimulation of the temporal lobes of the brain; some believe the latter causes experiences that resemble mystical or paranormal visions.

Blanke's work has been extensively quoted by the press as proving that out-of-body experiences are "all in the mind."[11] Yet a simple review of his work reveals that he is one of the key scientists relying upon the logical fallacy that producing a hallucination or illusion disproves something about the object of the hallucination or illusion. As I explained earlier, this is simply not the case. What Blanke's work actually shows is that the brain can be tricked or manipulated so that it becomes confused about the position of the body or limbs in space. It tells us little, if anything, about full out-of-body experiences. Furthermore, in a conversation with Dr. Peter Fenwick, a physician and leading expert on out-of-body and near-death experiences, he made it clear to me that Blanke's work "has never produced a proper out-of-body experience; he's produced [only] elements of it."[12]

The way that Blanke's research has been reported in magazines such as *New Scientist*[13] has been extremely misleading. Instead of giving readers an accurate picture of what is taking place in Blanke's laboratory, we are given the conclusion that OBEs are all in the mind, which the evidence simply does not demonstrate. I believe it is harmful to science in general, since this distortion in body perception has now been widely accepted by mainstream scientists as a valid explanation for OBEs, and led them to the conclusion that further research into the objective factors of OBEs is unnecessary.

Dr. Jeffrey Long, bestselling author of *Evidence of the Afterlife*, has clearly shown that the principal argument—that Blanke induced a classic out-of-body experience—is false. Long and his coauthors summarize the research by looking at two cases: an English patient who had a spontaneous out-of-body experience unrelated to Blanke's work, and a Swiss patient who was the key subject in Blanke's 2002 *Nature* journal article. Long's paper states, "[T]he English patient's experience seemed quite realistic, whereas the Swiss patient's experience was unrealistic—fragmentary, distorted, and illusory. In fact, a thorough review by one of us (Holden) of three classic books reporting extensive OBE research [Green (1968), Gabbard and Twemlow (1984), and Irwin (1985)] and one very recent review of the entire OBE research literature (Alvarado, 2000) reveals that the English patient's OBE is quite characteristic of OBEs in general, while the Swiss patient's is highly uncharacteristic."[14]

In conclusion, Blanke's work represents a totally artificial process using technology from virtual reality and brain stimulation, yet despite this elaborate approach, it has failed to reliably produce the results one would expect if the claim that OBEs are "all in the mind" is correct. Instead, he has produced less than what would be expected from, for example, a hypnotic induction with a suggestible subject.

James Randi

James Randi, a stage magician, author, and "debunker," is by far the most outspoken figure in the modern skeptical movement, and one source of its most common rhetoric. He is a complex figure. On the one hand, he is willing and able to actively expose charlatans and frauds, as he did with the Evangelical faith healer Peter Popoff in 1986. But there is another side to

Randi that many within the skeptical community may be unaware of, or choose to overlook. I believe that he is willing to blur the truth, and maybe even lie, when the goal of turning public opinion against the reality of psychic research is at stake.

For example, in 2000, Randi claimed in an article on psychic abilities in dogs: "We at the JREF [James Randi Educational Foundation] have tested these claims. They fail." He went on to say that a video of research done with a specific dog known as Jaytee did not show any sign of telepathy or awareness of when the animal's owner would return home. Randi stated: "Viewing the entire tape, we see that the dog responded to every car that drove by, and to every person who walked by." With this statement, he is arguing that the dog's behaviour was due to pure chance and nothing more. Yet according to Dr. Rupert Sheldrake, whose research Randi was referring to, "This is simply not true, and Randi now admits that he has never seen the tape." When Sheldrake challenged the claims Randi had made, Randi was forced after several e-mails to admit that his statements were total exaggeration. He wrote in an e-mail to Sheldrake, "I overstated my case for doubting the reality of dog ESP based on the small amount of data I obtained. It was rash and improper of me to do so."[15]

I shared the above situation not to make a particular point about telepathy in animals, but to illustrate the problematic nature of figures like James Randi, who is given a vast amount of respect by the skeptical community and continues to have large amounts of air time on television and in other media. It is important to ask why someone with such biased and reactionary views is given so much attention.

So how should we view James Randi's statements about other areas of psychic phenomena, including his claim that he has had an out-of-body experience, which was little more than a hallucination? When we consider what he says in light of his making repeated, untrue claims regarding Sheldrake's work, I find I am unable to trust the integrity of his statements in other areas.

We must proceed with a high level of caution concerning Randi's claim that he has had an out-of-body experience. During a lecture at Cal Tech in 1992, Randi described an experience in which he found himself floating "spread-eagle" on the ceiling of his bedroom, looking down at the large bed. He goes on to describe seeing his black cat curled up in the middle of the bed, while his physical body lay on the far side of the bed to avoid disturbing the cat. He also describes a grayish light that sounds somewhat similar to a common phenomenon within my own experiences, yet he seems to attribute this to a television set that is showing the static screen you might expect when there is no signal. He goes on to relate how the cat looked up at him with green eyes, which he remembers were the same shade as the bedspread. However, when he spoke to his adopted son the following morning, he found that the bedspread he had seen in the experience was in the laundry and the cat had been outside the house since four o'clock the previous day. In his lecture, Randi boldly proclaimed, "It was a dream, an hallucination if you will. It could not have happened."[16]

While this sounds like strong evidence against Randi's out-of-body experience, there are a few questions we should ask. First, was this an OBE as I defined it earlier in this book? Second, if it was, does this really tell us anything about OBEs? And last, is his conclusion logical? Following the logic used here—i.e., Randi's experience was false, therefore all OBEs are probably false—we could also conclude, to return to our earlier example, that a hallucination of a car flying past our upstairs window proves that cars are probably not real. This kind of reasoning is not workable and is based on a logical fallacy. We must seek out further evidence and explore further to reach a genuine understanding.

James Randi is not a scientist. He can tell us little about what actually might be going on in psychic and out-of-body experiences. He is interested in debunking frauds, which is admirable as far as it goes, but when it comes to science, we are better served to look to those who are doing genuine research that tries to answer our questions about paranormal experiences, not someone simply looking to fulfill his agenda by rejecting them.

   While skepticism is important and useful when approached without bias, the pseudoskepticism of many of those who are most outspoken about out-of-body experiences offers us little of benefit to our understanding of the phenomenon. I maintain that the best way to investigate the out-of-body state, and psychic phenomena in general, is through scientific methodology—not the opinions of of vocal individuals like Randi.

4

YOUR PERSONAL PROFILE: WHICH APPROACH IS BEST FOR YOU?

Having an out-of-body experience requires not a single skill, but a combination of skills. Just as learning to drive a car is not simply about being able to start the engine, learning to experience the full out-of-body state requires abilities ranging from relaxation, to visualisation, to letting go of fear or limiting beliefs. If any one of these factors is not in place, the result can be failure of the process. Before moving on to learning those specific skills, however, we must first identify which approaches to learning those skills are best for you.

In this chapter, we will explore the particular traits that make up your personality and lifestyle. Each one of us has particular interests and strengths as well as motivations and beliefs. By identifying these traits, we gain a clearer understanding of ourselves, which in turn helps us to identify the best approach for success in out-of-body exploration. When you understand your personality and abilities a little better, you can identify the most effective techniques to learn the key skills you need, such as relaxation or visualisation. All the techniques are detailed in the appendix, but please answer the questions in this chapter before reading ahead. You will find that I take a step-by-step approach to both the following questions and the techniques. The reason for this is so that you can learn new skills without focusing all your attention on the ultimate goal of having a fully conscious OBE. This approach removes some of the pressure you might feel by focusing overmuch on the end result and allows you to put your energy into fully learning each skill.

Your individualized program will consist of three main components: a relaxation technique, a vibrational state technique, and a range of techniques to actually leave the body. The determination of which components are right for you will be based on five key areas: your lifestyle, personality, relaxation, and stress level, as well as whether you are likely to be better at dream methods or conscious methods.

A Program to Suit You

In this section, you will find a series of questions designed to help you identify the best techniques and approaches for you personally. When completing it, I suggest that you make notes in a journal, although it doesn't have to be an actual book; it could also be a computer file. However, working with an actual book that you can add to and even make small drawings in is an advantage. Once you have a clear outline of what techniques you're going to use, you may also want to make a poster or "cheat sheet" with all the details laid out clearly for easy reference.

Available time

Obviously time is an important issue when starting this program. When will you do the exercises you will learn, and for how long will you do them? The ideal amount would be one to two hours per day. The minimum realistic amount would be thirty minutes per day. If you don't think you can spare this amount of time, consider looking in detail at your typical day and identifying a time obligation that could be reduced. Or consider using the Sleep Interruption Technique (see page 190), so that you can do your practice at a time when you would usually be sleeping.

How much free time do you have during the week?

Work out the total of free hours you have in an average week. Start with the number of hours you are usually awake and subtract time spent at work, commuting, preparing and eating meals, and so forth. Be realistic. If you have many distractions, your routine will suffer and your chances of success will diminish.

How much free time do you have during the weekend?

Do the same for the weekend. If you are extremely busy during the week, look for ways to give yourself more time to work on the program during your weekends.

Once you have an idea of your total available time, write it down in your journal. It's important to have a routine, so decide which blocks of available time you will dedicate to this program and on which days of the week. Make an appointment with yourself for these times and write them down in your calendar or day planner.

Waking, sleep, and dreams

I have found that generally people fall into one of two camps: those who are best suited to have OBEs from a sleeping state or during the night, and those who, like me, are able to induce the out-of-body state while waking. Finding out early which camp you belong to helps you to structure your program to best take advantage of your natural patterns. Once you have discovered whether you are a Type 1 person (waking/conscious) or a Type 2 person (sleeping/dream), you can begin to explore the specific techniques for that type. If your responses don't strongly indicate one type or the other, either approach would be equally effective, so simply choose the one that you are most comfortable using or the one you feel you would enjoy most.

How many hours of sleep is your optimum?

A. 6 to 8 hours (or more)

B. 4 to 5 hours (or less)

Do you have a regular sleep pattern?

A. No

B. Yes

Do you have vivid or lucid dreams?

A. No

B. Yes

Do you regularly have psychic feelings or impressions while awake?

A. Yes

B. No

Are you able to control your dreams at all?

A. No

B. Yes

Do you experience sleep paralysis?

Sleep paralysis is a condition in which you become conscious or awake while your body remains paralyzed, as if you were fully asleep. Some people also report seeing shadowy figures or feeling a presence, and/or sensations of vibrating or buzzing, which may have some relationship to the vibrational state experienced by some prior to an out-of-body experience.

A. No

B. Yes

Have you ever seen a ghost or experienced paranormal activity while awake?

A. Yes

B. No

———

If you answered mainly **A**, you are a Type 1 (waking/conscious) person. If you answered mainly **B**, you are a Type 2 (sleeping/dream) person.

The questions in the next section are designed to help you identify your personality type, and will further clarify which techniques may be most useful to you.

Relaxation

What level of stress would you say you experience in your day-to-day life?

A. High

B. Average to low

———

(A) If you feel that you have a high level of stress, for example, from a difficult or demanding job, you may wish to try the Presence Technique (see page 182) in your program. This will also encourage you to work on changing your reaction to stress in your daily life. You should also use the Deep Breathing Technique (see page 180) as part of your program.

(B) Please use the simple Deep Breathing Technique (see page 180).

Vibrational state

Have you ever experienced a feeling of vibrating, buzzing, or energy flowing through your body before or after sleep?

A. Yes

B. No

_____

(A) Try to remember the details: when did/does it happen most commonly? At what time of day or night? What had you been doing beforehand? How did you feel emotionally? Note these points down in your journal.

(B) Try not to have a preconception of how this state will feel; it is different for different people. Also, you may find that you can exit your body without experiencing it, so explore the methods for inducing it but just allow whatever happens to take place naturally.

Are you able to imagine or visualize well, such as in a guided meditation?

A. Yes

B. No

_____

(A) Use the Three-Dimensional Doorway Technique (see page 187) as your vibrational state technique.

(B) Work with the basic Introductory Vibrational State Technique (see page 186). Most people find this technique fun and easy to do. Also, don't get disheartened if the vibrational state does not happen right away, since it does usually take practice, and as I've said it is not necessary for everyone. However, do be aware that it is the most consistent way to have an OBE.

Personality

Are you more of an intellectual, visual, auditory, or physical person?

I have given examples below of types of activities that might characterise each type of personality. Select the one that you are most comfortable with or best at. This will allow you to find the technique that is likely to be most effective. If you find it hard to decide, you may want to think about your job, or your hobbies, or maybe ask a friend what category he or she would put you in.

Some people may find themselves unable to settle on just one category. For example, you might enjoy painting and consider yourself primarily visual, but you might also listen to lots of music and find that you respond strongly to the emotional impact of sound. You would then consider the visual as your main technique, but could also incorporate elements of the auditory approach, such as binaural beats.

- Intellectual (studying, computing, writing, debating, doing puzzles)
- Visual (art, photography, fashion)
- Auditory (listening to or playing music, listening to audiobooks)
- Physical (sport, camping, hiking, yoga)

Do you work better alone, with a partner, or in a group?

A. Alone

B. Partner or group

———

(A) Working alone to have an OBE has been the trend in most books, but there is no reason why it must be so. If working alone, you might find it helpful to develop a strong driving focus such as trying to reach a place where you have always wanted to go (or return to).

(B) As we are social creatures, I actually recommend working with a partner or even a small group. Developing a link to another person can give you the additional motivating factor of leaving your body to reach your partner. There are techniques in the appendix designed specifically for working with a partner.

Beliefs about OBEs

How do you feel about having an out-of-body experience?

A. Extremely positive

B. Excited

C. Positive

D. Open, but don't know what to expect

E. Nervous

F. Very nervous

In the next chapter, I deal at length with fears that may arise, but the important thing here is to really explore how you feel. Write out anything you think might be important in relation to the above question. Then, after trying the advice in Chapter 5, ask yourself the question again. Has your answer changed? As with all the questions here, use them as a starting point and enter as much information into your notes or journal as you feel might be beneficial.

Physical body

What is your level of fitness?

A. Very fit

B. Fit

C. Average

D. Below average

E. Unfit

F. Disabled

You may wish to get a health check before beginning your program, since some of the more physical techniques can be strenuous for those not used to them. If you have a disability, you may still be able to work with some of these techniques; again, it is best to get professional advice first.

If you feel comfortable that you are in the A or B category, then you will probably find the G-Technique (see page 200) particularly useful. People who answered C should use their own judgment as to what techniques might be most appropriate. If you answered D, I recommend the Sticky Hands Technique (see page 206), if you can find a partner to work with. If you fall into category E or F: unfit, disabled, or suffer from a health condition, I would recommend avoiding the G-Technique unless you are certain, after professional advice, you are up to it. If you take medication, especially pain killers, this might reduce your sensitivity. In this case working with the Sleep Interruption method might help.

For those with a previous out-of-body experience

What was the cause, if known?

A. I induced it consciously

B. Via a dream

C. It was spontaneous

If yes, when did it happen?

A. Before sleep

B. After waking in the morning

C. During the night

If you answered A, "I induced it consciously," how did you do so?

A. Visualisation

B. Sound technology such as binaural beats

C. Meditation

If you have had an out-of-body experience in the past, you can draw upon it to help with your program. Take a moment to think more carefully about your experience(s) and answer these additional questions:

1. Where did it happen? Was there anything unusual or interesting about that place that you could re-create?

2. How did it feel? Include your sensations, thoughts, and emotions in as much detail as you can. If you felt afraid, be sure to read Chapter 5, "Transforming Beliefs."

3. Were there any distinctive colours, sounds, or energies?

Look for ways to incorporate the elements you identified above into your personal program. For example, if you were burning incense when you had your OBE, try burning that same incense during future attempts (scent is a particularly powerful memory cue). If you induced the experience consciously, look for techniques that incorporate the method(s) you used.

Working with Your Personal Profile

You now have identified some key information about your sleep habits, health, psychic experiences, lifestyle, and fears. This will help you select the techniques that are best for you. Be creative and adapt them to suit you, especially if you have had previous experience with the out-of-body state. If you have never had an OBE, you will have a much better chance of success if you look closely at your personality and your needs. In the next chapter, we will explore the fears that you may have and how best to allay them.

5

TRANSFORMING
BELIEFS

In my experience working with people over the years, I have come to the conclusion that learning a few techniques for having an out-of-body experience is often not enough. Instead, we must understand the process that brings about an OBE and make changes in our lives to allow that process to take place. If we ignore the wider aspects of our lives, we will often fail in our attempts. Why? Because the way you view the world—what you see as positive, how you feel, and how at peace you are (or are not)—will impact the process on a fundamental level. That's why this chapter is called "Transforming Beliefs"—it is about understanding what might hold you back from having a full out-of-body experience and making the changes necessary. This will make your chances of success much higher. I have found that an unwillingness to change is the best indicator of those who will fail.

Some might find this confusing. After all, isn't the aim of this book to learn to have an out-of-body experience? What has how you live your life or what you believe got to do with it? The OBE is by definition an exceptional, or at the very least unusual, experience; therefore it requires a degree of stepping away from your comfort zone, away from the so-called "normal." If you stay within the boundaries of the everyday, you will only experience the everyday. Most people take the approach that they want to have an out-of-body experience, so they lie down and do some visualisation technique or other, and nothing happens. They then get on with their lives and say, "It doesn't work."

We must rewire our understanding of ourselves and what is possible, as well as deal with our fears, if we are to have regular and powerful out-of-body experiences. Limiting beliefs and fears of the unknown are key factors in distracting us from reaching our goals, not just when exploring the OBE but in the wider world as well. In my work teaching, I find more than anything else that fears based upon a lack of familiarity with the out-of-body state come to the surface again and again—especially when we are dealing with issues concerning "the other side" or the afterlife. This is because we fear dying or the experience of being outside of "ourselves." So in this chapter I am going to explore these fears, offer strategies to work with them, and give additional insights into the nature of OBEs.

What really takes place when we are in the out-of-body state is that we can realise our essential, or core, self. Our body is no longer the location of our understanding of what we are. We see that as Robert A. Monroe, author of *Journeys Out of the Body*, says, "We are more than our physical bodies."

For you, the reader, this book offers insights into accessing what I have come to call the transphysical levels—the invisible levels or planes, independent of the physical body, that are generally thought of as being subtler, more refined planes of existence. And what's more, as you learn to access these other levels, the OBE also offers amazing journeys anywhere in the universe. When you do experience the transphysical, you will see and feel levels of energy and forms of pure light that cannot even be imagined until you come into contact with them. The only thing that really stops people and makes the process harder is the fear already mentioned. One of the best methods to overcome fear is to familiarize ourselves with what being beyond the body really means and, by doing so, dispel myths and become increasingly more comfortable with how safe the practice really is. The previous chapter, in which you explored aspects of your personality, should have given you a clearer appreciation of who you are. The next step is to look at any limitations or obstacles that might prevent you from achieving a full OBE.

The Problem of Fear

Foremost among the fears involved with OBEs are the fear of losing control and the fear of bodily death. I believe they arise from the fact that we have nothing to reference when we find ourselves outside of our bodies; we cannot compare this state to anything else that we experience on a day-to-day basis, or even within most spiritual practices. For this reason, fears are normal but they can be transformed by building awareness. Part of this process is engaging directly with some aspects of your own fears. Consider for a moment your greatest irrational fear. Many people will say heights, spiders, or flying in a plane. Most of us have at least a mild phobia about something. Consider where it came from—what made you start to feel that way? You may find that it's not hard to locate a memory or event in your life that triggered this unreasonable way of thinking. Our fears about OBEs may be linked to childhood dreams or simply an overactive imagination. But they can also be linked to a fear of the paranormal. Even as adults, we see the paranormal constantly portrayed as something fearful and dark. This is related to the paranormal inaccurately being linked to the occult, along with the baggage of some religious doctrines. It is very easy to recall these references when we are alone in a darkened room, trying to connect to an unseen plane normally associated with the spirit or the soul.

These associations are unfortunate and can really hold some people back, but we must remember that they are purely the invention of Hollywood and fairy tales. The out-of-body state is actually energising, peaceful, and deeply spiritual, and has nothing to do with anything negative. I have spent much of my life in this nonphysical state and, as time has passed, I have become healthier, happier, and more compassionate. In short, OBEs have made me a better person. They can do the same for you.

To clarify these points, I'm going to address in depth some of the common specific fears people sometimes have.

Will you encounter negative entities?

This is an understandable worry for many people that I hear again and again, but I believe it is based on a slight misconception of how the out-of-body state works. I believe it is a misconception to view the OBE in terms of spirits or souls, and good and evil. Our understanding has moved beyond such notions in my opinion. Why do I view things in this way?

First, I have never encountered a negative entity during an OBE. This, I believe, is because we seem to be drawn to situations that are in line with our emotional and psychological make-up. If we are generally balanced and positive, then we will experience a balanced and positive environment. (I am not even convinced that negative entities exist, any more than I believe evil people exist. I see people in the world who do things I find morally and emotionally abhorrent, but I view this as the result of their circumstances and influences, not inherent evil or negativity.) If someone has a real concern about negative entities drawn from a particular religion or belief system, they should consider seeking support from their religious community or a counselor before attempting any of the processes in this book. The OBE in my view is a life-affirming journey of discovery into a world populated by light and wonder, not a world of darkness, shame, or demonic forces.

Can an entity enter your physical body while you are out-of-body?

The short answer, in my understanding, is no. As far as I'm concerned, the particular make-up of our consciousness only works with us. You could look at this as being similar to a fingerprint; it is unique to you, no one else has the same pattern. In the same sense, your body/brain's imprint is unique and no one else can "invade" this, any more than a person can jump into your body while you are physical. Just because you are on a higher energetic plane, in a finer form of matter, or your consciousness is extended (depending on how you view the out-of-body state), it does not change the uniqueness of your particular pattern or imprint. In my own OBEs, I have generally encountered other entities or beings in what seemed like a very physical body to me. It was just that we were operating on another level or plane. There was no way I could imagine them even accessing my personal space, let alone my body.

Both of the concerns above really derive from superstition about voodoo, witchcraft, exorcisms, and other misconceptions about the nature of consciousness and reality. I have focused on scientific approaches in this book in an effort to move away from these superstitions. As you have already learnt, science continues to reveal new information about the paranormal that can transform our understanding and allow us to let go of the preconceptions that may have held us back, such as the fear of demons and other dark forces.

Can you spy on people or can they spy on you while out of the body?

This is very uncommon in OBE reports, although there are instances of it happening especially through remote viewing techniques. Our innate desire for privacy seems to limit the ability of others to observe us psychically when we don't wish to be, and it creates a kind of psychic barrier or shield around our private emotions and activities. How this works is a mystery, but if an emotional connection is the key to success in psychical endeavors, as it seems to be, then it follows that a disconnection or block would have the opposite effect. I can think of only a couple of times in my life when I encountered a situation that seemed to contradict this notion of a psychic barrier. The first took place in central London, where I drifted through the wall of a large white building, almost mansionlike, not far from the center of the city. I came into a large lounge area decorated with very expensive furnishings, and as I moved through the space, a woman who appeared to be of Middle-eastern descent came into the doorway and stopped in her tracks. She seemed to see me! I must admit I was as surprised by this as she must have been and also froze, not sure how to react. She started to speak in Arabic, and raised her hands in the open-handed gesture of a Muslim prayer, as if seeing me as something of great spiritual significance. I was so startled myself that I fled the scene and phased back to my body.

Once in normal consciousness again, I slightly regretted leaving so quickly, but at the time I had simply not known what to do. Being seen was a whole new experience for me and I had no idea what it could mean. I researched apparitions of the living afterward, and even the concept of materialization, but was not able to be seen again. In a sense, being seen in this way can be frightening, as it brings the whole experience into the realm of objective reality again, and reminds us that this is not a dream but something that has a tangible effect in the world. It even makes you wonder if there could be some potential harm in becoming so physical that someone can see you. Yet despite these worries, I have never found any of this to be the case. The OBE is simply operating on a plane level that is unaffected by the types of things that would harm us in everyday life.

What if you can't get back to your body?

This is a valid concern—after all, the idea of traveling to locations across the universe is an amazing prospect, but if we can't return to our normal lives afterward, the appeal is obviously much less! Let me explain my own experience in a way that I think will address this concern. Since my first OBE back when I was a child, my main goal has been to extend the experience. I found that, as I left my body, I would immediately feel a sense of urgency, since I was well aware that the average experience lasts just twenty minutes. Some, of course, lasted much longer, but most would end very close to this time frame. I believe that this is due to the simple fact that our awareness is normally seated in the body and, whenever this is affected by an OBE or other altered state, there is a sense of the body or brain wanting to realign itself and return to the "normal way" that it functions and perceives the world. This reveals a key fact about OBEs: it is not hard to return to the body; rather, it is necessary to learn to maintain the out-of-body state for an extended period. Many people experience a kind of "pulling back" to their body or a simple phasing out, as if their consciousness is dissolving back into their body. My own OBEs tend to end with this fading of my consciousness from the exterior state to body awareness again. I have never once had trouble getting back to my body, even after many hundreds of journeys, and even to locations off this planet and outside this level of reality altogether.

Can you die if you are disturbed while out of your body?

This question goes back to the history of the out-of-body experience and its esoteric counterpart, astral projection. It was once believed that if your soul was not present in your body and you were jolted into physical consciousness, your soul connection (often referred to as the silver cord) would be severed and thus you would die. Fortunately, there is little evidence of this occurring. I can think of several instances when I was disturbed while my consciousness was outside my body, and the result was simply an uncomfortable return. The worst time I experienced this resulted in nausea for a few minutes, nothing more. Of course, it is best to avoid being disturbed if you can when doing your OBE practice, but it is not something to overly concern yourself with. Just take simple precautions such as turning off cell phones, asking those in your home not to interrupt you, and perhaps using earplugs as well as an eye-mask. This will increase your immersion in the process and reduce the discomfort that being abruptly disturbed may cause.

What if my silver cord gets severed?

If the silver cord exists (and I must admit I've never seen one), it is infinitely flexible and able to transform and become invisible, so there is little chance of anything happening to it, or to you. As I mentioned earlier, this book takes the most scientific approach I can give to the subject matter, and the existence of the silver cord does not fit well with the newer concept of OBEs being a form of extended awareness or consciousness. I will discuss this more later, but what is clear is that only a few people see a silver cord and it does not seem to matter at all to the quality of the OBE whether you do or not.

Are there any long-term side effects to out-of-body experiences?

My answer is no, assuming that you are in good health psychologically. I can see nothing negative coming from these experiences and, on the contrary, I've seen huge benefits. These include a greater sense of well-being, the fear of death dissolving, and the growth of spiritual understanding and awareness.

The only thing remaining is to look at your fears in a direct way and try to address them so that you have a greater degree of likely success in the OBE techniques. It is natural to feel fear when we are faced with the unknown or a situation that could spell potential danger. We must understand that fear does not stop us doing anything; we still have choices and we can learn to feel more comfortable with difficult situations. The familiar and the comfortable are not scary; in fact, for most of us they are a source of support and solace. So our goal when dealing with the object of our fear is to bring it from the realm of the unknown into the realm of the inspirational and supportive.

Many of us will have experienced fear when we have to speak publicly or perform in front of a large crowd. I remember my own anxiety when I first gave lectures and workshops; I would experience physical symptoms such as butterflies in my stomach and even sleeplessness the night before.

However, I learnt over time that I would always feel good after the lecture. I then learnt to focus on this aspect of the process. I also practiced visualizing myself up on stage in front of hundreds of people and I soon became comfortable there. The once-terrifying idea of having to stand in front of people and speak eventually became everyday, familiar, and actually enjoyable. I also learnt to be more comfortable with my fears as they became less important; after all, I knew that nothing negative was actually going to happen. I learnt to see my being on stage as simply having a conversation with a large group, which in my mind was no different from, and no more threatening than, having a conversation with a small group or one person.

Conquering fear is about shifting the way we look at the beliefs that we have. It is a process of exploring what the fear is and where it arises from. Usually we find that our fears are unfounded and that the situations we fear are actually opportunities for expansion, and can even be life-changing in many ways. In this sense, fear actually means opportunity—it is the signal that change is on the horizon, and that can be a very exciting possibility. You may want to seek out others who are also interested in OBEs as you learn to overcome your fears. You can join a group, attend lectures and workshops, or join an online community. These resources will give you greater knowledge and familiarity with the topic, and will also speed your development. Connecting with others with a similar worldview will inspire and motivate you. This sense of community is invaluable; feeling isolated is one of the worst factors for people trying to explore their spirituality. It should never be underestimated how important it is to have people we can turn to for advice and solace. Social networking websites too are growing in popularity every day; by using these tools, we can connect directly with those who share our goals. If there is no group or activity in your area, starting a simple group on a social networking site will allow you to benefit yourself and others.

EXERCISE: CONQUERING FEAR

- Step 1: Identify your fears.

- Step 2: Experience your fears.

- Step 3: Gain control of your fears.

Step 1 in this process is to identify your emotional reactions to the idea of leaving your body. How does the idea make you feel? You can start by making a "mind map"—a drawing of your ideas and how they relate to each other. In your journal, write down all of the emotional responses you have toward the idea of an out-of-body experience, reasonable or not. Really think about what you have learnt of this state of awareness. Do you feel any tension or discomfort arising? As you go through this process, explore these feelings further by creating a sub-branch of your mind map for each one. Try to look into the core of yourself: where has this tension arisen from? What is at the root of it? I often find that the limitations and blocks behind these feelings are never very far from the surface and can be easily explored in this way if you are honest with yourself and give yourself plenty of time to go through the process.

Step 2 is to experience these fears by really feeling the arising emotions. Don't suppress them; let them be fully realised, but as you do so, also step outside of them and view them objectively as an onlooker. Imagine yourself watching from a distance, like watching a play or a movie. How does this make you feel? Now take a moment to recognize the part of yourself that is outside of these fears, the part that is familiar with them but doesn't fear at all. There is always a part of you that is not engaged in the emotions of the mind—the observer. Now allow this clear, fully present part of yourself to become familiar. Before returning to your thoughts about the fears you've identified, ask yourself: do you feel different? Does your state of awareness now feel calmer, stronger, more relaxed, more centered? When we arrive at this awareness, we can more easily feel at home in these unusual experiences. We know from an emotional as well as intellectual standpoint that there is nothing but joy and inspiration in experiences beyond our bodies. Visualize the qualities and colours of your everyday self changing to those of the calm, peaceful observer self. See them now as one, and know that the fear was an illusion of the mind.

Step 3 is to gain control of the emotions surrounding your OBEs to transform them into powerful tools to propel you toward life-changing experiences. The best way to do this is through trance, the state in which we have access to the full range of our faculties. Richard Bandler, cofounder of neuro-linguistic programming (NLP), puts it like this: "Many people think that when you go into a trance you lose control of yourself; in fact, you gain control. You gain the ability to control your heart rate, your blood pressure, your ability to remember, your ability to use physical strength or dexterity, your ability to control time and your perceptions."[1]

Trance is simply a kind of mental focus, similar to meditation, which gives us access to our most powerful psychological resources. It is best not to concern yourself with what a trance is or is not, but simply to focus on the different aspects of moving your attention to your inner landscape. This will help with the wider goal of achieving OBEs, so trance is an important and useful tool to learn at this foundational stage of the process. Here's a short introduction to the process.

EXERCISE: TRANCE

- Step 1: Find a comfortable armchair or other suitable seat in which you can be totally supported, as you are going to reach a level of relaxation in which your muscles will be totally loose and free of tension.

- Step 2: We'll start with focusing on breathing; take a series of slow, deep breaths. Allow yourself to find your own rhythm, but deepen your breathing; breathe in and out with relaxed, natural motions.

- Step 3: With each outward breath, let go of all tensions and thoughts. As thoughts arise, become aware of them.

Sense their energy, sense where they have arisen from (work, relationships, etc.), and then see the colour and shape of the energy of that emotion.

- Step 4: Now return to the observer state of mind that you experienced in step 2 of the previous exercise, in which there is no fear. Let the energy of that safe space shift and change the colour and form of the emotion. Do this until you feel peaceful and still.

- Step 5: When you're ready, slowly bring yourself to full alertness while retaining the state of peace and awareness. You have now experienced trance: the state of being mentally focused, yet relaxed.

Apathy and Motivation

Apathy—the absence of passion or lack of motivation—can also have its root in fear, since we may avoid doing something precisely because we want to avoid succeeding. Apathy is actually the most common reason people fail. It is not that the fear of having an out-of-body experience is too much, or that the necessary skills are too complex; it is simply that most people do not put the techniques and skills they have learnt into practice, or they start but give up too soon. I have found that the longer we put hobbies or interests on hold, the less likely it becomes that we will return to them. When we feel hesitation or lack of initiative, we can learn to understand this as our cue to act, especially when we keep in mind that pushing ourselves into action is the factor that divides those who succeed from those who don't. We can inject some inspiration into the process to get things moving. If you feel that pinch of hesitation or avoidance, read something inspiring to motivate you, go over some of the techniques in the appendix, put on some music to create an atmosphere, but most important of all, learn to recognize this uncomfortable feeling as your cue to act. Many seek out a quick avenue to success, a shortcut that will allow them to avoid the potential stress of doing the practice. The irony is that I've seen many people spend more time looking for a shortcut than it would have taken them to simply undertake the steady process of development. People spend millions each year looking for a quick fix—a way to lose weight without exercise, become rich without work, or achieve spiritual awareness without practice. The reality in each case is the same: each requires change and dedication, and a set of simple yet effective skills. Success in life is never found through avoidance. It is found through a deeper understanding of our particular area of interest. Immersing ourselves deeply in a process, to the point that it is almost unavoidable, ensures that we will achieve some level of success.

Managing Your Time

We all have a limited amount of flexible time in our day-to-day lives. Many of us are almost overloaded with obligations. What does this mean to our spiritual well-being and growth? We cannot expect to find fulfillment if we spend many hours a day involved in stressful or tiring work and then spend only a few minutes to an hour or so exploring our spiritual nature. The sheer weight of outside influences is against us. To succeed in having on OBE, we must take time to focus on our spiritual and psychical development away from the stresses of work and family obligations. An extended workshop, a period of meditation, or a retreat are all helpful ways to balance the weight of our commitments. Spending time focused on ourselves and our goals in this kind of nurturing environment is an excellent way not only to rebalance ourselves, but to reconsider our life choices. Much like a positive change of diet or stopping smoking, a change in the way we utilise our time can improve our emotional and physical well-being.

If you feel that you need to address this time issue to allow more time for this program, start by allocating just fifteen minutes a day to your practice. (Anyone can squeeze fifteen minutes out of his or her day!) Another tactic is identifying a negative or limiting element in your life and either ending it or reducing it down to a manageable level. Common time-wasters that take up more time than actually benefits you include surfing the

Internet aimlessly, watching television, reading articles that offer nothing, or wasting time, money, and energy shopping. Whatever your sources of mindless distraction, become aware of the amount of time spent and seek to reclaim some of that time for something nurturing and life-changing, like a spiritual practice.

When I teach, I often find that people underestimate the amount of time they really have available. They feel overwhelmed, and just thinking about making changes brings up anxiety. It is important not to allow this attitude to limit you, or to become the reason that you don't see this program through. If you have a computer, smartphone, or diary, set a reminder each day to take time to work on yourself. Just fifteen minutes a day can change your life. As was mentioned earlier, working with a partner can also help to motivate and engage you. In short, it is important to find time within the structure of your particular job and commitments that lets you reclaim something for yourself.

EXERCISE: IDENTIFYING YOUR DISTRACTIONS

Distractions are a part of our daily life, and becoming aware of them is the first step toward overcoming them.

- Step 1: Write down a list of topics that you thought about or discussed with friends or family today.
- Step 2: Next to them, list where the ideas came from: what led you to be thinking about that topic? Start with the morning and the first person you met: what did you talk about? What led to the conversation? Did you think more about that topic, or explore it further, later on?

Let's use my day as an example. I woke up and soon thereafter my partner started talking about the death penalty. This topic arose because she was reading a book as part of a course of study on ethics. So the source for this conversation was education—information from an academic source. The next person I spoke to was a friend who spoke about a documentary on mediumship he had watched the night before. So the second source of information was television.

- Step 3: Become aware of how sources outside of yourself impact your thoughts and your time.

When I do this exercise, it is amazing how often the trail leads back to visual media such as television. The workplace and education of some form are also common. Very little is from self-initiated sources for most people. This is what I advise you to change. Look at the influences in your life and reduce passive sources where the choice of what you learn or think about is not your own. Reduce exposure to topics that you have not drawn to yourself, and increase exposure to topics that you wish to learn about. Consider skills you'd like to learn and pursue them. Engage with spiritual writers who inspire and motivate you, and explore the fields that will lead to a greater understanding of your psychical faculties. This is key when wanting to gain the most in your learning about OBEs and the nonphysical levels. You cannot develop advanced abilities and understanding in a vacuum or with no positive or nurturing influences. You also cannot make progress without the simple investment of your time.

6

IMMERSIVE APPROACHES TO HAVING AN OUT-OF-BODY EXPERIENCE

With this chapter, we will begin to explore the specifics of having an out-of-body experience. First we will look at the impact of the environment—specifically, the effect of special types of environment designed to fully immerse yourself in the experience. These "immersive approaches" are highly effective ways of inducing an OBE through the use of several or all of the senses, rather than just one, as is common in many approaches.

The term *immersion*, in the context that I use it here, is mainly drawn from the world of virtual reality (VR), which is an attempt to create a believable experience of a computer-generated, artificial world through the use of headsets, three-dimensional (3D) glasses, and other technology designed to trick the brain into believing that what it sees is real. There are two common forms of VR immersion. The first utilises a head-mounted display that plays a slightly different version of the virtual world into each eye, with the resulting illusion of a three-dimensional space. The second form does not use a head-mounted display; instead it creates the illusion using a "cave," which is a small white room onto which images are projected. When the cave is viewed through simple 3D glasses, the effect is that you seem to be physically within whatever environment is being projected.

While VR technology has mass appeal when applied to entertainment, it also has constructive applications, such as its use to help people with phobias. Within the safety of the artificial world, a person suffering from, say, fear of spiders can gradually desensitize himself or herself and release his or her fear response when confronted with a real spider.

Like VR technology, the field of sensory or perceptual deprivation also uses the idea of immersion. In the 1960s and earlier, several laboratories were studying the effects of various forms of sensory deprivation to determine what psychological impact it might have. Immersion was used in a literal sense: participants were submerged into tanks of water, usually in total darkness, to see what would happen once the senses were in effect switched off. This resulted in a whole array of hallucinatory experiences. It was also around this time that scientists studying psi abilities such as telepathy began to experiment with mild sensory deprivation to help people get successful results in psychic trials. This is where immersion really becomes applicable to our aims. Immersion has two powerful factors: first, it can impact the part of the brain that helps us understand the world around us in a way that can help us grow or overcome fears. Second, it can help us to get deeper into our unconscious awareness, which can aid psychic development.

Robert A. Monroe was the first person to explore a mild form of immersion using a system of sound frequencies he named Hemi-Sync®, based upon the binaural beat concept first put forward in 1839 by Heinrich

Wilhelm Dove. The idea, in simple terms, was to use sound to alter the brain state of the person listening to the frequencies. Monroe discovered the concept while exploring the possibility of using similar technology to enhance learning. Instead, he had his first out-of-body experience.

While Monroe's system was ground-breaking, it was limited to sound alone. In 1998, I began work on my own immersive system designed to help induce an altered state. But unlike Monroe's, mine would involve all the senses to create a complete sensory experience, thus greatly increasing the impact on the participant and the chance of having an OBE. I have continued to develop and refine my approaches, and in 2004, working with a designer/curator and an artist, I built an immersive environment at London's Science Museum that used sound, 3D film, and VR technology to take the idea of immersion to the next level. Next, I will introduce the ideas behind these cutting-edge developments and explain how the reader can create a simple immersive system at home.

My Experiments with Immersive Environments

My first project exploring immersion as a way of accessing the out-of-body state was called Epicene. It not only allowed me to get solid feedback from participants on what worked and what didn't, but also allowed me to help people experience totally new states of awareness in a very safe and effective way.

The idea for the piece had been with me for a long time, and I sketched out many ideas before finally creating the plans for the project. My early versions were more like hammocks, after I had experimented with an ancient approach called the "witch's cradle," which is basically just being suspended from a tree in a sack. I had read about it in some of the literature on astral projection, and found that the intensity of the experience did lend itself to inducing OBEs, but obviously its discomfort meant it would not be for everyone. I wanted to find a way of inducing a similar psychological impact without making people feel uncomfortable.

I began to think about floating. How could I make someone feel as if he or she was weightless? It occurred to me that if I could build a structure that would respond to the slightest movement, as well as visually seem to be floating, maybe people could experience a sense of weightlessness. I soon began to formulate how the structure could be built, and luckily at the time I had access to a workshop where I could actually build it.

Physically, the piece consisted of a large metal frame, cube-like, with a white, bed-like platform suspended within by steel wire (the kind used in theatres to suspend actors above the stage). A participant would lie on the platform, which gave a feeling of floating. As he or she relaxed, a recording would begin playing, much like a guided meditation. First it would guide them into a highly relaxed state, then it would begin to take them into a light, positive trance state. As they became more deeply involved in the experience, they would be guided through a series of scenarios that would introduce possibilities, such as leaving the body, on a fully conscious as well as a subconscious level.

The results were often deeply emotional and people would find that they had accessed a part of themselves that they were almost totally unaware of. There was a sense that the experience could potentially open people up in a similar way as going through months of practicing visualisation techniques.

Almost as soon as I had a good level of feedback from people about their experiences, I began work on my second project. This time, I wanted there to be more than the hypnotic induction; I wanted to use light as well. I had been thinking a lot about the possibilities of virtual reality. At the time, I didn't have access to the level of technology needed to make a fully immersive VR system, but I did have a good enough understanding of technology to set up something similar.

The result was a project I named LAM. It consisted of a computer that ran a lighting and sound system, as well as video projectors showing footage designed to suggest that consciousness is fluid and not limited in the ways we often assume. I did this by showing more generally understood concepts, such as the "self" watching the world from inside one's head in a visual form, and then showing the senses disappearing or being reduced and posing the questions, "What is left? Where is the 'I' located?" This is actually a very hard question to answer and it poses the further question, "Is consciousness an illusion?" This does not mean that consciousness does not exist, but rather that it may not be what we believe it to be, or it may not work in the way we think. This can be very liberating, as it opens us to explore the nature of our consciousness. It suggests to those who may never have considered it that we may be more than our senses, or maybe that "I," wherever it is located, could be capable of much more than we ever considered.

To truly open up to the possibilities of consciousness, we first must relinquish our preconceptions and limited worldviews and be open to new possibilities. Using the benefits that technology can offer is one way we can experience new ways to reach other levels of consciousness.

The Ganzfeld Approach

The Ganzfeld Approach is a form of mild sensory deprivation that was introduced into psychology in the 1930s. It was later taken up as a tool by parapsychologists studying telepathy. The real effectiveness of this approach is that it gives us a relatively easy way of taking our attention away from our external senses and encouraging a connection to our unconscious mind so that psi perceptions can come to the fore.

The process begins by taking two halves of a Ping-Pong ball and placing them over each eye to shut out all visual input (thus creating a "total field," the meaning of the word Ganzfeld). The brain is then encouraged to become active by the use of a red light, dimly visible through the ball halves. This causes the pupils to dilate and the brain to look for incoming information from our physical senses. When nothing comes in, the brain begins to fill in the void and we start to hallucinate. This effect is enhanced by the use of pink noise, which is essentially the random static that you hear if you tune a radio to the frequencies between stations. After a time in this state, psi impressions can come to the fore in a far more reliable way than if you were simply closing your eyes.

In psi research, a person in another room, called the sender, will try to project or transmit images to the person in the Ganzfeld state. The sender is usually looking at a series of images that have been randomly selected. These are usually images of major landmarks or other easily recognisable subject matter. When the experiment is over, the person who was in the Ganzfeld state (the receiver) will be asked to look at the random images and also to listen to a recording of the session. He or she will be asked to choose the image that they feel the sender was trying to telepathically transmit.

The Ganzfeld Approach has produced some of the most powerful demonstrations of telepathy under controlled circumstances.[1] It has been replicated in many laboratories worldwide in accordance with scientific protocols. The results are especially compelling in the auto-Ganzfeld variant, which uses a computer to control all elements of the experiment, thus greatly reducing any chance that the receiver could gain knowledge of the target image in any physical way.

The Ganzfeld process is extremely useful to our goal of inducing OBEs because it helps to bring about a trance and takes you to a deeper level of inner focus. It is also useful to those who are uncomfortable or unfamiliar with being in a trance state; you will be able to take your first steps with the help of a tested system that is also pleasant to experience. I have found that this system, when combined with the vibrational state and other techniques, enhances your chances of having an out-of-body experience. Furthermore, it requires only a set of headphones, a Ping-Pong ball, cotton wool, tape, and a red light (the kind used in photography darkrooms is ideal).

When working with any form of sensory deprivation, the experience is best kept fairly short, especially at first. This is because extended periods in sensory deprivation have been shown to cause anxiety and stress. Although this is highly unlikely with a mild approach like Ganzfeld, which commonly results in a sense of peace and expanded awareness, for general well-being I recommend a period of no longer than thirty-five minutes to start. It usually takes around fifteen minutes for people to reach a trance state in which visual impressions form; these experiences then generally last for around twenty minutes on average, for a total of thirty-five minutes, which is the ideal period.

How to make your own Ganzfeld system
What you'll need:

- A Ping-Pong ball

- Fine sandpaper or a nail file

- Cotton wool

- Tape (medical tape is good)

- A sharp knife, such as a scalpel or craft knife

- Headphones and something to play pink noise (see my website at www.grahamnicholls.com for a 35 minute pink noise track)

- A red light

- A comfortable seat or recliner

With the knife, carefully cut the Ping-Pong ball into two halves. Gently place them over your eyes, taking care not to cut yourself with the edges, to get a sense of where you might need to shape the sides to better fit your face. Once you are happy with the fit and you can see virtually no light, take the file or sandpaper and smooth the edges off.

Next, switch on the red light and sit or lie down. Experiment with your position until you find the best distance that results in a uniform reddish glow coming through the Ping-Pong ball halves. When you're ready to start, place some cotton wool under the edges of the ball halves to make them more comfortable and improve the fit. Then apply some tape to hold them firmly in place. The tape can also block any areas where light is getting in.

Now put on the headphones, start the pink noise, and relax. It may be helpful to use a relaxation technique like focusing on your breathing. Pay particular attention to any sense of the vibrational state arising, or any energy sensations that come to the fore.

After around fifteen minutes most people start to see images, colours, and impressions arising. Go with these and try to enhance them and be fully present with these impressions. For example if you see a field of grass, try to see it vividly and try to sense the temperature or smells around you. In short, try to be there.

Once the pink noise comes to an end, take a few moments to ground yourself, before removing the headphones and Ping-Pong halves.

Make notes of what you experienced and try to recall how you felt, especially if you got to the vibrational state, as you can draw on this to reaccess the state in future.

When and How to Use Immersion

Immersive approaches are not techniques, in the literal sense, to leave the body; they are designed to plant the seeds for a later experience. The more we suggest to our unconscious mind that we wish to leave our bodies, and the more emotionally and powerfully we do this, the greater our chance of success. My system, Epicene, can lead to a full OBE, and the same is sometimes true of the Ganzfeld. However, by working with these mild forms of sensory deprivation, say in the early morning, you will experience the benefits when you use other techniques, such as before sleep, for example. It is one part in the overall process of turning your attention away from the mundane aspects of everyday life, opening up your innate psi abilities, and filling your awareness with the vast potential of the out-of-body state. We have to train ourselves to give up our preconceptions and allow new influences that offer growth and creative awareness to impact our psychology.

It should be highlighted again that extended sensory deprivation or immersion is not desirable. Since it can become stressful, those of a nervous nature or those with any health concerns should consult a professional before working with these approaches. In fact, even if you don't have any underlying issues, I advise that you only use it twice in any week, because more often could reduce the possible benefits. The use of sensory deprivation should be approached with respect, awareness, and balance. If your use of it becomes unbalanced, it can result in unnecessary stress. You should also stop using it if you experience any form of anxiety.

Some research suggests that using any form of immersion is more effective during the very early hours of the morning, between two and four. This seems consistent with the experiences reported by religious practitioners for centuries. The work done by Michael Persinger, discussed earlier, shows a relationship between brain function and the mystical states described by all cultures. Persinger uses a device nicknamed the "God Helmet," a specially adapted sport helmet that stimulates the brain using a magnetic field in such a way as to produce experiences that closely resemble numinous or religious experiences. His work can be considered similar to immersion, although the idea of direct brain stimulation in this way seems less appealing as a methodology for me.

Concerning Hallucinogens

We need to be fully aware of the safety of any system or practice, including the point at which we no longer feel comfortable. This is, of course, a personal decision, but careful consideration is necessary since some approaches are not fully tested and we are unaware at this point what impact they could have on general health. For this reason, I have never used hallucinogens and other forms of drugs in pursuit of mystical experiences. The relationship between OBEs and other mystical states may suggest to some people that the use of drugs might be beneficial, but I have concluded that the mixing of these two areas is not advisable. I have seen many people who have fallen victim to psychosis as a result of mixing drug use with altered states of consciousness such as the OBE.

Some hallucinogens are thought to produce experiences similar to the OBE, such as ketamine, *Amanita muscaria* (fly agaric), and *Hyoscyamus niger* (henbane). While these can produce profound experiences, I strongly advise not using this approach. Most often the experiences produced by hallucinogens and other drugs are uncontrolled and don't include many of the more objective elements of the out-of-body experience.

Hallucinogens may offer a wider insight into the possibility of other levels of reality, which can be useful for those who have not experienced the out-of-body state and other transcendent experiences. However, if you follow the processes in this book, you will find that you can gain greater understanding and control of your psychic potential without the risk associated with powerful chemicals.

If you have already worked with these drugs, you will no doubt be aware of their potential, and you may now benefit from an approach that reaches higher levels of awareness without further use. My own spiritual approach is focused on learning to be more aware and engaged, so I believe it's more beneficial to learn skills rather than simply taking a drug. However, I do recognize our environment as a key factor in what shapes and defines us. This leads me to believe that where we live and the influences we draw upon leads to the understandings we have. The immersive approach in this sense is a realisation of the importance of our sensory stimuli. While we cannot avoid some forms of influence, we should be very careful about what we consciously choose to bring into our lives.

Other Forms of Immersion

Flotation tanks, which were popular a couple of decades ago, are rarely discussed today. They can be very effective in relaxing the body, reaching a sense of limitless space, and reducing your awareness of your body. There are flotation tanks in most major cities, and they can be found by a simple search on the Internet. You can also create a similar setting in your own home. All that is really needed is a normal bathtub in a darkened room, with a high level of Epsom salt in the water. Epsom salt has a long association with health and vitality. It has different properties from other "salts," since it contains sulfur and magnesium. It is made from a rock called dolomite, which is found in the region of the Alps known by the same name. Dissolved in water, it has the effect of making the body more buoyant.

The basic process involves entering a small room that is free of light and noise and floating in a pool of highly salted water for a period of time until you reach a heightened or relaxed state. This process is often accompanied by soothing music or sounds such as whale calls.

Controlled Holistic Environment Chamber (CHEC) units, developed by the Monroe Institute, also offer a sense of being separate from the everyday world and offer the mental and physical space needed to engage with your inner state. Once inside, sound technology, such as binaural beat audio tracks, would be played via headphones, slowly taking you into an altered state, or focus, as it is sometimes known. For some this is a highly effective way of inducing an OBE.

There are also ways to create a do-it-yourself, multisensory system at home using 3D glasses, surround sound, and even virtual reality technology for home use. Some of these tools can be used as an add-on to other methods. The simplest method is using a television or computer that can play video. I call this the Aerial Footage Approach (see page 192). First, find some footage of something suggestive of being out-of-body, like aerial footage taken from a plane or helicopter. This is easy to find on the Internet and gives a strong suggestion of flying and moving awareness to the unconscious mind.

Sit back in a comfortable recliner or chair and put on the footage, either in silence or with some basic music or sound. Watch the images flowing over the screen and try to transport yourself there. Don't just see the images; try to feel the sensations you would feel if you were actually experiencing what you're seeing. Remember, this is a form of suggestion or affirmation—you are trying to communicate to your unconscious that you are comfortable in this state and that you want to experience full and controlled out-of-body experiences. Try to spend at least an hour or so watching the footage. The more you can saturate your awareness with the idea of weightless, limitless movement and freedom, the more likely it is that you will have an OBE when you try some of the more active techniques.

The Aerial Footage Approach is especially powerful when watched standing up. You will probably find that when doing so, your body will begin to sway. Your muscles will start to react to the visual stimulus, making the experience even deeper. This effect can be further heightened by reducing the lights or using a projector, if you have access to one, so that the images take up your whole field of vision.

Many of the approaches I am sharing in this book work best in combination with other techniques, so after using the questionnaire from Chapter 4, it is best to select the approaches for each stage that are most suited to you personally, and work with them consistently. It is generally not a good idea to keep changing approaches, unless you find a particular technique ineffective for you after a minimum of, say, a month. The impact that particular approaches will have is very subjective and depends on your psychology. For instance, some people find Ganzfeld a little strange or alien, while others love it. The same is true of the Aerial Footage Approach. I have found that Ganzfeld is better for people who are more kinetic or physical in nature, while aerial footage is excellent for people who enjoy a more visual experience. By all means experiment, but remember that consistency and a degree of discipline are important to success.

Traditional immersion systems

As well as the many modern, technological forms of immersion, there are many forms that have been used in tribal cultures for centuries. Even a temple or church can be viewed as a form of psychological immersion. Although it doesn't have the element of sensory or perceptual deprivation that I usually include in my definition of immersion, it does surround the participant in sound in the form of music, visuals in the form of art, and even smell in the form of incense.

In Native American communities, processes such as the sweat lodge were and are used as a way to immerse those taking part in a mild ordeal with the intention of releasing psychological issues and purifying the body and spirit. Using heat to purify was also one of the symbolic meanings of the sauna in Finland and Estonia, where the sauna was considered sacred.

As with all forms of immersion, those used by pre-technological cultures were designed to push the body to an extreme of some form so that the mind would be free of chatter and mundane concerns. This results in mental clarity and a state akin to meditation or other practice designed to still the mind. It is also possible to experience some sense of this through physical endurance or sexual activity. For many people, orgasm is the only way that the chatter of the mind is dissolved temporarily. In practices such as some forms of Western Tantra, immersion in sexual intercourse and related practices can lead to transcendent states of awareness.

Physical sex can actually be a useful technique for achieving OBEs (as differentiated from "astral sex," which I'll discuss later). The most powerful approach is to maintain the point just before full orgasm for an extended period. If you go through the techniques for visual people outlined in the appendix, you may find that the sexual dimension and work with a partner will increase the energy and impact of the approaches. Understanding the physical body's limits and strengths is a real advantage in learning its relationship to the nonphysical state. In the next chapter, we will explore how a greater understanding of your body will give you real control of your OBEs.

7

THE PHYSICAL
BODY

Our state of awareness and our well-being define the nature of our experience on Earth. This is also true when dealing with the out-of-body state. Within states of heightened sensitivity, nonlocal perceptions become more likely. Perceiving from beyond the confines of our physical senses takes place most commonly when we are in a critical condition, as in the case of classic near-death experiences, but also when the body and mind are tuned to a high level by a light, nutritious diet, regular exercise, and mental techniques such visualisation. All these things move our awareness away from the coarse sensations of everyday life and allow us to shift more easily into an altered state of consciousness such as an OBE.

The first and often most powerful change we can make to impact the physical body is to our diet. It is virtually instant and offers ongoing benefits for our health and well-being as well as our spiritual awareness.

Diet

A vegetarian diet has long been recommended for spiritual seekers. I believe this is due to an awareness that paranormal experiences are easiest to achieve when the body's energies are not taken up by the digestion of heavy food not ideally suited to our physiology. While humans are generally described as omnivores, this is essentially an observation of our habits and behaviours; it has little to do with the way in which our bodies work. In fact, our facial muscles, jaw, mouth, teeth, saliva, stomach, small intestine, colon, liver, and kidneys all suggest that we are naturally plant and fruit eaters, not carnivores or even omnivores.[1]

An awareness of our vegetarian physiology has huge implications for our health, since meat and dairy products have been shown to cause or contribute to a wide range of diseases, including many cancers and heart conditions. The most extensive study ever conducted on the subject is outlined in *The China Study*, a book by Dr. T. Colin Campbell, a professor of nutritional biochemistry at Cornell University. Campbell was so compelled by the findings of the twenty-year study, undertaken by Cornell University, Oxford University, and the Chinese Academy of Preventive Medicine, that he removed all animal products from his diet and became vegan.

Campbell's findings are not surprising if we take into account the fact that our bodies are not naturally suited to diets rich in animal fats and proteins, yet in the Western world we generally consume large quantities of these substances. I have found that a diet rich in raw foods with no products derived from animals is the most suited to my physical well-being and my ability to attune myself to the subtle levels needed to have out-of-body experiences.

I first experimented with becoming vegetarian during a retreat at the age of sixteen. The changes were immediately apparent as I found that my awareness of usually unconscious emotional ties, needs, and sensitivities became clearer. I also found that my sleep was impacted by the diet change; I could sleep deeply and my dreams became more vivid. That year was also the last time I visited a doctor with anything other than a sport-related injury. I virtually never get colds, and feel that my immune system is supported by what I put into my body, rather than undermined as it was before I became vegetarian.

I took the step to veganism several years later and again felt improvement in my physical and mental condition after clearing myself of energy-depleting foods. Dairy's effects are in many ways worse than meat. It has opiate-like effects, making people who consume it regularly susceptible to cravings. Cheese especially is high in fat and lactose, which many people, especially those of African origin, are intolerant of.

I recommend that all animal-derived foods be removed from your diet if you seriously want to attune yourself to out-of-body exploration. While experiences can be achieved on a meat and dairy diet, we are making the process harder by putting our bodies under pressure.

There is also the ethical issue of eating meat and dairy products; like many people, I believe that so-called food animals suffer at all stages of their use. If we understand that consciousness is interconnected and nonlocal in nature, then what are the implications of consuming a product that contains the attributes of abuse, fear, and death in every cell? The ethical concerns related to veganism are hugely important to any understanding of spirituality or metaphysical ideas about how we are bound to all other life. We agree as a society and as individuals that morality helps to define us as humans. It seems logical to extend this moral understanding to all life; animals have a desire to live and avoid suffering in the same way that we do. It is not enough for us to say that, because they do not have an evolved sense of morality, we can therefore ignore our own morality.

When we begin to understand our interconnections with all life and practice compassion, we extend the possibilities of how we can extend our consciousness. We free ourselves from being bound to the psychic suffering of others and create a more harmonious set of possibilities for our spiritual future.

Optimal veganism

I hope I have made a concise yet clear argument in favour of veganism and its benefits to one's psychical and spiritual well-being. But I want to go further in my explanation of veganism to explore the best way to eat to benefit every area of life. A diet free of meat and dairy, if not done properly, will not give the kinds of benefits that we want to achieve. The body must be nourished with fresh, whole ingredients. Foods are often most beneficial to us in their raw state, especially fruits of all kinds. Foods that fall within the category of fruit include the ones most of us are aware of, such as apples, oranges, and bananas, but there are many more not generally thought of as fruit. One example is nuts, which are excellent for giving the body what it needs without weighing it down or reducing the flow of energy around it. Green leafy vegetables, such as spinach and kale, are also excellent nutrient-rich foods that will not burden the body. These can be juiced or added to a fruit smoothie if the flavor of the raw greens puts you off. I have found that when added to a smoothie in this way, you barely notice that the greens are present. Another low-cost, highly nutritious food is hemp seed. It can be ground to a powder with a coffee grinder and sprinkled onto other foods or added to smoothies. There are many other highly nutritious foods that do not burden the body. I would advise you to do your own research and look into what works best for you.

There are also many ways to create raw versions of your favourite foods, leaving you feeling fresh and not overly full. One of my favourites is a raw vegan version of a tomato and basil pasta. In place of pasta noodles, cut thin strips of zucchini with a slicer or peeler. Chop a few large tomatoes, some fresh basil leaves, and a small amount of garlic and onion. Blend the ingredients with seasoning to taste, pour them over the zucchini noodles, and add olives, olive oil, and a few more pieces of torn basil leaf. The result is a really delicious meal. To enhance the basic recipe, you can also add sprouted seeds, nuts (ground or whole), and nutritional yeast, which is a vegan source of many of the B-group vitamins. There are many more recipes like this available online and in books, all of which help to promote optimal health and maintain energy levels for OBE training.

Fasting

Reducing or going without food for a period of time is one of the oldest spiritual disciplines. I recently heard an experienced expert on fasting say that it is not necessarily the fast itself that is the most powerful aspect of the process, but instead it is the point at which we begin eating again that really has the greatest impact. This is because, after a period of abstinence, our relationship to the food and to the impact of the food on our body has changed. We become aware that the energy from that food is being utilised by the body. We can literally feel the sensation of our body transforming the food into energy, and our relationship to food may never be the same. Rather than seeing food as simply a sensual pleasure with no deeper implication, we come to see it as the sustenance for our whole spiritual being. We learn to see our mind, body, and spirit supported by what we put into our body; we make a link between how we experience the world and what we do to our body.

It is, of course, best to seek medical advice when considering any type of fast, and it is also a good idea to have someone present throughout the process for support and in case of any issues that may arise. Fasting is a generally safe practice, but it is best to be cautious and not take any unnecessary risks. Many books are available that go into far more detail about the process than we have room for here.

If you're inclined to try fasting, I suggest that you start slowly with a juice or soup fast. Once you feel more comfortable, move on to a water-only fast, starting with one day, then two days, and eventually a few days—but no more than this, as it becomes counterproductive if you push yourself beyond a few days. It is extremely important to drink liquids constantly during a fast. During a juice fast, you will replace your usual meals with a nutrient-rich juice or smoothie. I recommend that you focus on the dark green, leafy vegetables and fruits mentioned earlier. I would start with a two-day fast, making sure that you have a good variety of (preferably organic) fruits and vegetables easily available. You will want to keep your fluids high, so at least a liter is ideal for each sitting. For a smoothie, I recommend using a selection of berries, such as blueberries, raspberries, and sea-buckthorn berries (if available), plus bananas for a thick, smooth base. I also often include celery and spinach. Of course, there are many other variations you may wish to try, and many recipes for blended juices and smoothies are available in books and on the Internet.

A soup fast is basically the same as the juice fast, but instead of juice you eat only soup. If you take this option, be sure that you don't opt for a soup that contains large solid vegetables; it should be a light blended soup that will act in a similar way in the body as juice or a smoothie.

Physical Exercise

As we all know, diet is not enough to attain optimal health; we must also exercise regularly. There are many ways to approach this, depending upon your current state of health and your interests. Practices that offer a low level of stress for the body, but which also condition and promote a sense of well-being, are best suited to our goal. Yoga, as well as some of the Japanese and Chinese martial arts, fit well into this category. Any practice of the physical yogas, such as variations of hatha yoga, is best accompanied by pranayama, or the yoga of breathing. Like yoga, tai chi has been known for generations to benefit body and mind as well as to enhance the state of mental stillness that is ideal for leaving the body.

If these Eastern approaches do not appeal to you, there are many more ways to achieve the well-being that will benefit your OBE practice. Hiking and climbing, for example, are beneficial because they combine a high degree of spatial awareness and a connection with nature, while at the same time strengthening the body. This is the core of what someone looking to develop nonlocal perception in general, not just OBEs, should be looking for. Any practice you choose should prepare your body for the mental disciplines of consistent practice and awareness of your relationship to your environment. The more you can move away from the distractions of modern living and engage with what your body is telling you, the better.

A couple of years ago, when I was living in East Sussex in the south of England, a friend and I decided to do a thirty-mile hike across the local area. We set off in early morning and didn't reach our destination on the coast until well after dark. When we finally made it back home, my body felt almost numb from the miles of walking cross-country and over several large hills along the coast. I lay there, my mind in a heightened state quite unique to this level of exertion. Moments later, I felt waves of soothing energy that felt much like the sensation of warm sunlight on the body, before I lifted out of my body and up through the roof of my house. I could make out the deep grayish-purple of the nighttime sea in front of me and the lights dotted along the curve of the coast in the distance. I let myself be drawn toward the lights and the delicate clouds on the horizon before drifting off over the countryside to unknown parts of the area.

I believe that experience was brought about by a day of engaging with the landscape and pushing my body to a state in which my mind became paramount. The usual concerns of my body, such as food and comfort, were placed into the background, while my consciousness came to the fore. It is an extremely liberating state of being and, even without the out-of-body aspect to the story, it shows why people are drawn to push themselves in their physical activities. We reach a sense of our own core self; we have taken control and defined our wants for ourselves.

For many people, their bodies may not be capable of the kinds of activities mentioned here. The important thing is to cultivate the notion of wellness and deep relaxation or physical calm. If this can be achieved, the OBE can allow those with physical disabilities or limited mobility to experience a level of freedom that cannot be achieved through any other method I am aware of. For example, there are many cases in the literature of near-death experiences of blind people suddenly being able to see when out of their bodies, or people normally unable to use certain limbs having the ability to do so.

Relaxation

Relaxation is of central importance to success in out-of-body exploration. In the context of OBEs, the goal is to separate your mental activity from your body awareness. For most people, these functions go hand-in-hand; when someone is physically tired, they are also mentally tired. For that reason, mentally taxing or stressful areas of life are more detrimental to the process than physical exercise. There are some minor exceptions to this, however, like when you are extremely emotionally heightened. Nerves, emotional longing, and excitement are examples of this. You may be tired in any one of these states and unable to relax, but still in a good condition to have an OBE. Perhaps surprisingly, a state of physical exhaustion actually can be conducive to OBEs, provided you are not also mentally exhausted. This reveals that the use of the word "relaxation" can be a little misleading; many people assume relaxation to be a completely passive, inactive state, although it doesn't have to be.

Some readers may actually be unaware of what a true state of relaxation is, but there are tools that can help us identify what is going on inside our bodies. For example, biofeedback devices measure physiological responses, such as electrical activity in the skin, for the purpose of bringing these responses under one's conscious control. These devices are essentially a way to get feedback from our bodies. The first one of these devices I ever owned was a very simple plastic dome that you held in your hand with two of your fingers in contact with metal plates on the surface. This allowed the device to pick up the subtle electrical signals in the skin and turn them into a tone that you could hear through simple headphones. As you listen, you can relax your muscles and alter your breathing until the tone begins to grow lower and lower, until eventually it stops. You would then be in a highly relaxed state.

I learnt a lot from that little device about basic relaxation and understanding the tensions in my body. There are now much more advanced versions on the market that use neuro-feedback, which monitors brain activity rather than simply electrical activity in the skin.

Brain waves and neuro-feedback

Understanding brain waves and their effect on your brain state will allow you to effectively control your state of being in ways that general meditational practices take years to yield. The known brain waves are delta, theta, alpha, beta, and gamma. Alpha waves relate to a brain frequency in which both relaxation and mental focus are present; the alpha state is highly apparent in experienced meditators. Entering an alpha state using meditation or biofeedback can help with overcoming fear, as discussed earlier. It can also be an excellent tool to cultivate alongside whatever relaxation technique you decide to use in your program.

Theta waves are often associated with enhanced learning and may also be effective for some aspects of OBE training, but at this time it is unclear whether this approach is useful. One of the issues is the lack of a clear definition when OBEs are referred to; some researchers categorise the out-of-body state as being the same as a lucid or conscious dream, while others put it into the same bracket as remote viewing. This can be confusing, because while these types of experiences seem to be clearly related, they are generally much milder than an OBE and take place without the full sense of separation from the body—without which we are blurring the line of what constitutes an OBE to an unhelpful level, in my opinion.

Nevertheless, training yourself to enter different states of awareness using neuro-feedback or biofeedback devices gives many benefits that will support your OBE program. If you have the resources to explore such devices, I recommend it; however, it is important not to rely on it as your sole method. Some people find that an approach using sound frequencies or binaural beats alongside neuro-feedback is effective in inducing OBEs, but many others only experience a state of relaxation or a "spacey" feeling. This may be most effective for those who rated as a more auditory person in the questionnaire in Chapter 4.

Sleep

Many people find that an OBE is easier to achieve from sleep, usually by waking up outside of your usual sleeping routine and practicing a series of techniques at that time. The fact that you are already in a half-asleep state means that part of the relaxation side of the process is already in place. Some also report that they can induce the vibrational state more easily at this time, and that the visualisation techniques are easier. However, elements of sleep paralysis may also sometimes be present.

The most relevant fact about sleep paralysis is that it can cause a state of awareness while the body is essentially still sleeping. For this reason, if you have undergone something like sleep paralysis, you should definitely explore using the Sleep Interruption Technique of leaving the body. To most effectively interrupt your sleep, use an alarm system that does not jolt you abruptly awake. There are many variations available, such as wrist-watches that vibrate and alarms that use gradual increases in volume or light to wake you up. Some devices even claim to monitor the stage of sleep you are in and wake you up either in deep sleep or during the dreaming phase of sleep. You can also easily use an ordinary alarm set to its lowest effective volume.

If you are waking up to do your practice at a time when there is daylight in your bedroom, I advise that you use a simple eye mask. Daylight can lead to you becoming too awake to gain any benefit, and also the eye mask will make it easier to do your visualisation techniques.

While I don't advocate sleep deprivation for an extended period, a small amount can be useful. You may wish to try staying awake much later than you would normally, or even for a twenty-four-hour period, and then go through your OBE programme hourly. There is some danger of falling asleep when you do this, but if you can remain awake, you may find that some of the energetic techniques become easier. Your sensitivity may be raised and, if you're working with a partner, you may find that perceiving his or her state of awareness is much easier. I've found that the period between 2 a.m. and 4 a.m. is an excellent time to practice and experiment.

Sound

Sound has a huge impact on the human state of awareness; I believe this is why monastic communities across the world have used sound-based practices as the cornerstone of their traditions for thousands of years, and continue to do so today. A few weeks ago, during a gathering at my home with a few friends, I picked up a singing bowl, the type used by Tibetan Buddhist monks. I began to play the simple brass bowl and almost instantly the entire room's energy changed; the people became quiet, and they shifted their attention to what I was doing. This is just one of many examples I could give of the power of sound to impact human awareness.

Singing and chanting are probably the oldest forms of using sound to change our state of consciousness. I particularly like chanting, since it requires no instruments or special skills, simply the voice and a willingness to experiment. There are, of course, more advanced forms of chanting, and the practice of overtone chanting in particular can be very effective, but merely using the voice in a rhythmic pattern can be powerful. It is liberating and even cathartic to express yourself in such an unlimited way. I advise you to start by allowing your voice to make any sound that feels good to you—your own unique language, so to speak. You can change the tone and close your eyes and go with the sound. You can increase and decrease the speed as you practice. You may find a natural rhythm that leads to a useful technique for changing your state of awareness. If you find you enjoy chanting, you may wish to explore more structured chants or complex techniques.

Music, when focused on religious or spiritual awareness, can set in motion those same shifts in consciousness. Many classical compositions, which expand the imagination through complex beauty, have a similar effect. I find that listening to the sounds of the planets can transport me in my imagination in a way that can be suggestive of an OBE. These sounds are actually radio waves emanating from the planets in our solar system, which are then converted to sound. They have an otherworldly quality about them, and they also have an added benefit to our goal of working with the out-of-body state—they make us focus, even if unconsciously, on the vast expanse of space and the areas that we can reach, at this point, only via the out-of-body experience.

More conventional forms of music can also be used to expand the imagination and develop our awareness. But it is sound, especially when produced by our own bodies or very simple instruments, which seems to hold the greatest potential. Simple repetitive rhythm supplies a basic framework for our minds to project onto. This expansiveness of mind leads us back to the very core of what the OBE is about: it leads us away from the everyday experiences and the limited understanding that surround us, and leads us toward the realization that our consciousness can reach to the planets and stars and maybe even witness the birth of the universe itself.

8

THE EXTENDED
MIND

From the time that our earliest beliefs about the world around us were formed, human beings have proposed the idea that within each of us is a spirit or soul. This spirit is generally described as having much the same qualities and appearance as our physical body, but it is made of some mysterious form of energy and it appears to survive bodily death. In this chapter, we will explore what this means in relation to the out-of-body state.

Most books on OBEs assume the existence of an astral, etheric, or other kind of subtle body. In this book I want to avoid such assumptions as much as possible—not because there is something wrong with these ideas, but because we have the possibility of learning something new when we look with fresh eyes. This chapter is about asking questions and examining what you personally experience without preconceptions. In the past, I've held beliefs about the out-of-body experience that hindered my progress; before we move on to practical matters, I want to help you avoid such limitations.

So let's start by exploring the question: Does the subtle body, promoted by the adherents of Theosophy and other traditions, exist? Or does the theory of the extended mind, briefly explored earlier, provide a better explanation for the out-of-body experience?

What Is the Subtle Body?

In modern writings on the subject, some theorize that the spirit or energy body could be made up of "dark matter" and "dark energy." Dark matter/energy is a mysterious substance that some claim makes up 90 percent of the universe, yet it is all but invisible, since it does not give off light nor absorb light.[1] It exerts gravitational force on visible matter, yet atoms are unaffected by its influence. This offers a fascinating possibility: that physical things, such as our brain and body, may have a "dark" or invisible copy. This sounds very much like a spirit, and that is exactly what some parapsychologists have put forward as a possibility.

I first came across the idea in a book entitled *Shadow Matter and Psychic Phenomena* by Gerhard D. Wasserman. For many years, this seemed a beautiful connection between modern physics and the OBEs I had been having. Then, as I explored the idea further, I came across the work of Rupert Sheldrake and his theory of morphic fields. Sheldrake has spent many years exploring whether evolving fields of influence exist, and showing that our mental processes are not limited to the inside of our brains.

In Sheldrake's work, however, the notion of a subtle body becomes less important, since he believes that biological fields form from activity and evolve over time. He sees the "laws" of nature as being more like habits. This has many interesting implications for the out-of-body state, since there is little doubt that the second body is very fluid and closely linked to consciousness in a way more suggestive of a kind of field than an invisible, dark-matter body.

The search for physical evidence of a soul or spirit body existing beyond death is a long one. In 1907, Dr. Duncan MacDougall published a paper detailing a series of experiments that involved weighing a body at the time of death.[2] MacDougall believed strongly that if continuation of consciousness after death took place, then it must be via a body of some form. He writes: "If the psychic functions continue to exist as a separate individuality or personality after the death of brain and body, then such personality can only exist as a space-occupying body."[3] His conviction was based on his understanding of the science of the day—that there must be a form of "gravitative matter" as the basis of the "soul substance," as he called it—but could he prove such a notion? He set out to weigh the physical bodies of a range of subjects, shortly before death and shortly after, to see if there was any difference. If there did exist a body that included some physical mass, as he believed, he should be able to detect it, assuming its mass was not too small for ordinary measurement devices available at the time.

He describes his first subject as a man dying of tuberculosis, selected because the nature of his disease would cause little bodily movement, which would have disturbed the weighing process. His method was simple, but far from precise by the standards we expect today. MacDougall states: "The patient was under observation for three hours and forty minutes before death, lying on a bed arranged on a light framework built upon very delicately balanced platform beam scales."[4] He goes on to describe the actual moment of death: "At the end of three hours and forty minutes, he expired and, suddenly coincident with death, the beam end dropped with an audible stroke, hitting against the lower limiting bar and remaining there with no rebound. The loss was ascertained to be three-fourths of an ounce (20 grams). This loss of weight could not be due to evaporation of respiratory moisture and sweat, because that had already been determined to go on, in his case, at the rate of one-sixtieth of an ounce per minute, whereas this loss was sudden and large, three-fourths of an ounce in a few seconds."[5] MacDougall went on to weigh another six subjects at the time of death, resulting in a perceived average loss of weight of 21 grams, a figure that has now entered the popular imagination, due in part to a recent film by that name.

From a scientific perspective, MacDougall's experiments were too loosely controlled and open to tampering, so they can't be held up as strong evidence of a soul or spirit; even so, his results have continued to fascinate for over a hundred years. Our obsession with the notion of a soul or spirit has not diminished with time, but is the soul composed of a physical substance, as MacDougall theorized? Personally, I think it is unlikely.

What Can We Learn from Personal Experience?

As mentioned at the beginning of this chapter, I think it's important that you examine without preconceptions what you personally experience. In this section, I'd like to share what I've experienced during my OBEs.

Most researchers agree that, if there is an actual body rather than a framework of consciousness, then it is a very malleable and fluid body able to take on an array of different forms. This suggests that consciousness is the guiding principle behind the form; in other words, our awareness defines how we experience our form. This is backed up by my own experience. Sometimes I lift out of my body to perceive my "self" as a radiant point of awareness, full of light; on other occasions, I perceive having a body, with all the normal characteristics of my physical body. It seems that when a body has some role to play in the OBE, such as standing at a location or touching another physical object, the body form or field becomes apparent.

For example, on several occasions I have made a connection to a physical object while out of my body; I have done this simply by touching it. Once, when I touched a flower, I was aware of my slightly energised hand touching the delicate surface before I felt transported into the very cells of the plant, which felt like many points of consciousness spread out like a small universe, yet also existing as one. I could feel myself present in every cell, as if each one was an individual but intimately linked to a grand network of life. Both within the plant itself and within the ecosystem of the forest around me, the delicate play of energy, water, and light seemed perfectly balanced.

In another experience, the sensation of touching a door was fascinating in a different way; I experienced the inside of the hollow wooden form. I remember the tiny splinters of chipboard inside the narrow enclosure between the two surfaces. The layers of paint were also visible, as my perception could focus closely on any element of the structure. I felt only the vaguest sense of resistance from the physical form of the door; it was as if my awareness was fully interwoven between its atoms. We can see, in both of these examples, the interplay between my awareness of a body and my experience of pure consciousness.

There are many in the scientific community who believe that the way we experience the world—our consciousness—is not simply a process of unaltered sensory information coming into our brain. Instead, they believe that much of how we actually experience consciousness is the result of the mind filling in the gaps that our senses leave. I am not just talking about minor optical illusions and the like. The idea is essentially that the old notion of a stream of consciousness is the result of the piecing together of various sensory fragments to create what *appears* to be a congruent whole. This implies that consciousness itself is a kind of illusion—not that it doesn't exist, but that it is the result of many elements coming together to form something that appears to be whole and seamless.

If this is the case, it could mean that when we experience fragmentary imagery and shifting perceptual awareness in psychic and out-of-body imagery, maybe we are actually experiencing a purer unfettered consciousness, free from the interference of the brain. As mentioned earlier, psychic and OBE perception has much in common with memory; it is often emotionally driven, which means that we generally remember what was important or powerful to us. In a similar way, in psychic perception, we become nonlocally aware of that which is powerful on an emotional level.

If we break all this down, our out-of-body and psychic awareness resembles a mind without the brain creating the theatre of the mind—or the simulation, if you like—that we know as our consciousness. This is not a negative concept, since "illusory" in this sense only means that there is a deeper level to our experience of the world, and that the OBE can give us direct contact with that level.

This idea has much in common with the concept of Maya in some Eastern traditions. Maya means "illusion" and represents the notion of duality. In other words, we believe ourselves to be separate from everything when, in fact, everything is one. In this sense, there is no distinction between self and the universe as a whole. Maya represents a state of awareness that can be transformed through spiritual or psychological development.

It seems that the further we extend our consciousness through practices such as the OBE, the closer we come to the notion of consciousness as a kind of movie playing out our emotions, thoughts, and needs, dissolving into a state of oneness. We discover that consciousness is simply not what it appears to be. The more we remove our preconceptions about the nature of things, the more likely we are to break free of the illusory and embrace the real core of our awareness.

Cosmic Consciousness

The idea of cosmic consciousness, or the interconnectedness of all life, can be traced to the beginning of the last century, just a few years before Duncan MacDougall began his experiments with the weight of the soul. This was a unique period in history when the birth of many new ideas was transforming the way we looked at the world. Charles Darwin's theory of evolution was well known, but many were slow to champion natural selection as its primary process. Albert Einstein published his theory of special relativity, and within a decade Carl Jung introduced the concept of the collective unconscious. In fact, Jung's idea of a kind of psychic store of information containing elements of our ancestral past has much in common with Richard Maurice Bucke's writings from this same period. Bucke envisioned three stages in the evolution of consciousness: the first is the animal, or instinctual level, followed by the ordinary human, and then, finally, the cosmically or universally aware and evolved state.

It could be that cosmic consciousness is, in fact, a state of awareness in which the collective unconscious becomes accessible; the collective unconscious becomes the collective consciousness, so to speak. Whatever the case, Jung's and Bucke's theories were and are an attempt to look in a scientific and progressive way at the transformative psychic experiences that people have. The twenty-first-century idea of the extended mind is a refining of these concepts in a way that brings it into line with the findings of parapsychology, yet it has all of the same possibilities.

In the theory of cosmic consciousness, we find the notion of a network of thought that is ultimately aware. In a similar way to how the individual neurons in the brain are thought to lead to the complexity of our minds, each mind becomes a part of a greater whole. Quite early in my own OBEs, I experienced something very close to this interconnected mind. I had been reading about the astral planes and the idea that there is a whole array of other levels of reality that somehow coexist with the world we perceive with our everyday senses. While these other levels are invisible when we are physical, they become accessible while we are out of the body. This idea fascinated me; I wanted to know how far these levels extended, if indeed they had any limit at all.

As I closed my eyes and went through the process of becoming aware of my energy, I focused my attention far above the room in which I was lying. Within moments I felt myself lifting up; I remember the distinct sensation of moving through the ceiling of the room above and, a few moments later, the sensation as I turned to move through the wall of the building. Then, as if all the barriers had been removed, I moved straight up with a force that seemed almost out of control. Soon the familiar, winding, cobbled streets and distinct landmarks of London disappeared and were replaced by points of energy and form. It was as if I was seeing the underlying structure of things; the heavy, immovable world of physical matter was now replaced with swirling energy and vivid colour like nothing on Earth. I don't know how I got there, but it was as if, by moving almost faster than the speed of light, everything had collapsed around me to reveal its true nature as some kind of primordial light from the source of the universe.

I was dissolving into this maelstrom of infinite possibilities, and my self, my understanding of me that had been everything to me a few moments before, seemed unimportant in this moment. For an instant it was as if I was losing control, and I paused as if I wanted to return, but a second later that last egotistical resistance disappeared and I was somehow everywhere and everything.

In a burst of true cosmic consciousness, I saw what appeared to be the birth of the universe in such unbelievable motion that it seemed to turn in on itself, like it was moving backward and forward at the same time, because time itself was not yet born. In each new moment, it was as if every aspect of my being became unified with the totality of everything. I moved faster and faster with the expanding universe until I reached the point where the whole process paused, before I too turned in on myself and seemed to become a single tiny point encompassing everything that is.

Then I felt myself reforming into some semblance of myself, like the first embryonic cell separating to eventually form a complex life, my life. Moments later, I was looking at my physical body; somehow it seemed to contain the map or route that I'd taken in that experience. It was as if I was looking at my current state of evolution that I had seen beginning just moments before. Often in my OBEs I would barely recognize my body; it would seem like seeing a stranger in the street or lying asleep, as if it wasn't anything to do with me somehow—but tonight it was. It represented my journey and the form through which I was able to learn and grow to the point of experiencing this cosmic understanding of the universe.

That was only one of many experiences I've had in which I was able to glimpse the power and magnitude of the universe. Although each time I have returned to some level of normality afterward, these experiences on other levels and in a state of cosmic awareness have changed a part of me forever. I can't say whether I was aware of this during those experiences, but now when I look back, I can see how my life went in new directions each time I experienced the real power of the OBE to expand my consciousness.

Even my awareness of this planet has increased in profound ways. I can perceive a planetary awareness or consciousness that arises from all of life and the delicate balance of the Earth. While out in nature, or experiencing an OBE in a distant location, I would often sense that there was some kind of awareness behind the beauty of the mountains, rivers, and vast planes of this world.

The Global Consciousness Project

I am far from alone in experiencing a sense of the conscious nature of the planet. But there has been little attempted in the area of science to investigate how our thoughts, emotions, and beliefs might impact the nature of awareness worldwide. The Global Consciousness Project, founded in 1998, is the first wide-ranging attempt to look at how human attention might be linked across the planet and what this might mean.

According to its website, "The Global Consciousness Project (GCP) is an international effort involving researchers from several institutions and countries, designed to explore whether the construct of interconnected consciousness can be scientifically validated through objective measurement. The project builds on excellent experiments conducted over the past thirty-five years at a number of laboratories, demonstrating that human consciousness interacts with random event generators (REGs), apparently 'causing' them to produce non-random patterns."[6]

Like many of the ideas we explore in this book, the Global Consciousness Project has huge implications for our beliefs about the underlying nature of spirituality, as well as the importance of our thoughts and actions. This relates directly to the "law of attraction" and the exciting possibilities of quantum physics. Whether or not theories like the law of attraction are "real," they stem from the growing understanding that consciousness appears to be linked and able to interact with matter. Even if this is only on a very subtle level, the work of organisations like the Global

Consciousness Project adds another important piece in the puzzle that attempts to explain the possibility of life after physical death, the existence of telepathy, and even our ability to change the flow of our lives through our thoughts and intentions.

The way that we think, and the level of awareness that we attain, have long been thought to impact the nature of our reality. In my understanding, global consciousness—also called the extended mind—is part of the mechanism that allows for out-of-body experiences. Like an Internet of accessible awareness that stretches in every direction, it enables us to tune in to a vast resource of information, as has been used in recent years by remote viewers. The Global Consciousness Project provides yet another piece of the converging evidence that demonstrates the extended mind is a reality.

The Extended Mind and Enlightenment

Enlightenment is generally seen as a very grand term, one that is hard to define, yet what we do understand of it seems in tune with the idea of the extended mind. Enlightenment implies a state of detachment from the concerns of the ego, a state of awareness in which consciousness is fully engaged in the self. This is not the self in the sense of "selfish" wants or desires; it is the true self that exists when the stuff of everyday life and the ego has been stripped away. In short, enlightenment is about fully realizing the nature of ourselves as we truly are, and within that is a sense that the divisions we see between ourselves and others are an illusion.

The idea of enlightenment has much in common with the extended consciousness of the out-of-body experience or any spiritually transcendent state. The OBE is not just a way of having a powerful experience; it is quite literally a step toward a deeper spiritual understanding (and maybe even the fabled enlightenment). The implication of this understanding is that the OBE will change you, if you allow it. It can bring about a greater sense of peace, compassion, and even comprehension of others, quite simply because you start to see others in the light of your own self. You stop seeing all life as separate and begin to see even the darkest and most fearful aspects of our humanity as the result of a rational cause; therefore you may find that the desire to condemn or judge others vanishes. I feel that the OBE has made me view the negative traits and actions of others as arising from a cause lying within the personal landscape of the person involved, and while I may avoid his or her negative behaviors, I do not see the person as "evil" or in need of punishment.

That which is spiritual, literally speaking, means "relating to the spirit or self," and the spirit or self refers to the psyche or the mind. In the past, the spirit and the mind were generally seen as one. The very notion of the extended mind inevitably leads to questions about the nature of spirituality because, in many ways, the extended mind as a concept is a modern form of that age-old notion of the mind and spirit being one, or at least arising from the same source. Thus we come full circle to an understanding of spirit as an interconnected consciousness able to exist outside of space and time. So what does this mean to someone about to leave his or her body for the first time? What might you expect to find and experience, and how might it change your way of viewing life and death? In the next chapter, I will explore these questions and try to give some sense of what might unfold as you travel deeper into your own psychic landscape.

9

LEAVING THE BODY: WHAT CAN YOU EXPECT?

I have described some experiences I've had when my consciousness, or self, was beyond my body, but what can *you* expect to experience when leaving *your* body? To answer that question, let's look at what we know of the nature of the experience itself rather than drawing upon myths, traditions, or superstitions.

Whether or not the mind is local to the brain, as discussed in Chapters 2 and 8, the OBE undoubtedly owes much of its nature and characteristics to our emotions, memories, and senses—essentially the elements that make up our personal interpretation of the world around us. When we have an OBE, these key elements of ourselves appear to be projected to a distant location, in some form. How we then interact with that location is dependent upon these elements, by which I mean the particular set of emotions and awareness that makes up our individual personality or consciousness.

It seems highly likely to me that the subtle differences in OBEs from one person to the next are dependent upon the way in which our particular personality interprets the world. In everyday situations, such as going to work or spending time with family, the impact of our consciousness is less obvious, but in an OBE, the way that our consciousness is focused and balanced defines how we experience every detail. There is, of course, common ground; virtually all of us have emotional bonds, loving relationships, and people with whom we feel deeply linked. This shared human experience forms the most powerful psychic links and has been shown time and time again to be an important factor in psychic experiences. For example, there are many documented accounts of someone suddenly becoming aware of a loved one in danger, sometimes even before the event has taken place. These experiences are so common that nearly everyone has heard at least one example. In psi research, too, people with a strong emotional link have shown that they can successfully connect with each other's thoughts or impressions, and they can do so far easier than strangers or those who know each other only in passing.

In my early OBEs, I would virtually always find myself in my bedroom, just a couple of meters from my body. In my present-day experiences, however, I generally find myself at a location many miles from my home. I believe this is due to the change in my understanding of the experience and also how I emotionally relate to the world. In other words, the framework of my emotional make-up and my consciousness has changed over time and thus my experiences have also changed. In my teenage years, my perception of the world was very much supported by my family life. I have always been very close to my mother and father and even had a strong bond to the flat in which I grew up. It is no surprise, then, that this same psychological framework defined where I would find myself once out of my body. The colours and feelings associated with my earliest experiences also seemed to be an extension of my limitations and unconscious fears and beliefs. These subjective factors to the out-of-body experience can also be seen in the near-death experience.

But are there elements of an OBE that are consistent for all people? The answer is that there are elements that are experienced by *most* people. For example, vibrations shortly before exiting the body are a very common occurrence; however, these vibrations are not always described in detail, so it can be hard to ascertain just how consistent the sensation actually is. In my own experience, the sensation is closer to a wave flowing through my body, often accompanied by a feeling of starting to be separate from my body. I am still aware of my body at this point, but I start to sense that my perception is becoming less "localized." This wavelike feeling builds to a point at which I sense I am almost physically somewhere else. I then begin to see my environment; this sometimes requires me merely to open my eyes.

The Vibrational State

In Robert A. Monroe's book *Journeys Out of the Body*, we find that his first description of the vibrational state sounds quite distinct from the one that I have just given. He relates how a beam of light appeared in the sky above him: "I thought it was sunlight at first, although this was impossible on the north side of the house. The effect when the beam struck my entire body was to cause it to shake violently or 'vibrate.'"[1] In his technique for leaving the body, he also describes the vibrational state as almost violent in nature. For me and many others, this is not the case, so while this sense of vibrating energy is common, the form it takes is different for different people.

I have found that those who work with the emotional factors of their psyche before the vibrational state arises will more often than not experience a more peaceful form of this energy. It seems that those who are more materially focused in their lives, such as those with a high-powered job or those involved in the sciences, can experience a more intense form of energy.

I must emphasize that this is not a negative thing; it is simply that this type of lifestyle may be more stressful and therefore requires more engagement with the process of relaxation. In the same sense, those with highly analytical mindsets may require a greater engagement with the subtleties of the vibrational state. Overall, lifestyle and emotional make-up impact many elements of the out-of-body state.

The process of actually leaving the body is also highly influenced by one's emotional state and level of relaxation. Once the vibrational state reaches a peak, a sense of separation usually follows. This can sometimes take the form of a very physical exit, where the experience while out of the body is much like normal physical reality; in other experiences, there can be a total absence of physical elements.

My first encounter with the vibrational state was probably the almost-violent jolt I experienced the first time I induced an OBE. Although I didn't view it as such at the time, it had many of the characteristics of the vibrational state, but compacted into a single burst of energy that resulted in me floating a few feet above my body. Over the months that followed, I began to sense a calmer, more fluid kind of vibration, one that felt as if I was being gently lifted up on the crest of an invisible wave. This process would culminate with me shifting, or as some put it, "phasing" to another place. I would usually only start to see after I had already left my body. I didn't see myself lifting free and still don't. I might see colour or feel a sensation of shedding my body, much like slipping off a heavy coat. To this day, this is accompanied by a sense of release, a very pleasant feeling of being energised and being free of any stress or tension present in my physical body.

Once out, I could open what felt like my eyes, although I never sensed physical eyelids; it was more like using the same process or mental signal to look, and I would feel my eyes focus in some form and images appear. I would then see my surroundings in many different ways, from forms of energy and light to physical structures with the same colour and layout as normal everyday reality.

Encounters Beyond the Body

Many people ask me if I encounter other beings while outside of my body; the answer is yes. Sometimes I encounter others who also seem to be having out-of-body experiences. At other times, I come into contact with people who appear to have physically died, and at still other times, I encounter beings who appear to be from another plane of reality altogether.

When I have seen others who are also having OBEs, our ability to communicate depends on the degree to which our awareness is in sync. This communication is more of a telepathic link and sometimes is based more on feelings and visuals than on the conventional idea of communicating through language. For this reason, what language you speak is unimportant. You experience the inner motivations and needs of the person, not the sounds that they make. I don't know to what degree this is an objective form of communication, but it does seem that at least the sense of what is felt is transferred to the other person. All in all, I think it is easier to transfer emotions or a sense of deep connection rather than literal words. This seems in line with the kinds of connections seen in telepathy tests in the laboratory. The depth of the relationship you have with the person you encounter is key. I have, of course, met strangers in these OBEs, but so far I have not been able to verify these by meeting the person in physical reality. I am interested in whether this could be done, because if so, it would really offer another powerful piece of objective evidence for OBEs.

People's appearance within an OBE does not seem to coincide with their normal everyday appearance. It is usually more of an energetic form, much like the idea of the aura. Rich colours flow through their humanoid form, and often their features are obscured. I believe this may have to do with the level of consciousness needed to sync with another person energetically—in other words, when you are attuned to the person as an energetic form, you see or sense their framework of awareness rather than everyday impressions of the person. However, this does *not* seem to be the case with people who have physically died. In this case, the person will often appear, at least to you, as they did while they were physically alive, right down to the clothes they are wearing. Why this might be is a mystery; we can only surmise that it could have something to do with what we want or expect to see.

Sex and OBEs

Several books on the subject of astral projection contain long discussions of the possibility of "astral sex." Three types of sexual union have been referred to over the years. The first and most arcane form is called *congressus subtilis*. This form derives from the occult writings of authors such as Aleister Crowley and describes the subtle, or second, body drawing substance from another person's physical body whilst experiencing some form of sex. Crowley describes this as having much in common with descriptions of *incubi* and *succubi*, or sexual demons, believed by some to prey on individuals in order to steal their vital energy.

However, the stories of sexual demons visiting people during the night sound virtually identical to descriptions of sleep paralysis. They usually entail the person involved being unable to move, while a figure, creature, old woman, or man climbs onto their chest. So clear is the link between sleep paralysis and the incubus/succubus stories that much of the literature on sleep paralysis refers to them at some point.

Creating a connection with the physical body of a person remains highly unlikely, in my opinion, despite Crowley's statements that "The one really easy 'physical' operation which the Body of Light can perform is 'congressus subtilis.'"[2] However, he does not give an example of his experiments in this area, and I must say that I remain unconvinced. Having said that, I have experienced a form of "presence," which I was able to verify with a sexual partner the next day. The two most powerful examples of this involved sensing an energy body in the bed with me for the entire night while no one was actually present. This was not merely a vague mental impression; it was the sense of an energetic form being present, to the point that I would turn on the light and try to see what was there. When I spoke to my partner the next day, she immediately mentioned her awareness of us being together the entire night despite being miles apart. This is an experience that many people report, which seems to suggest a kind of telepathic link was taking place. I wonder whether this could be built to such a point that a sexual connection could be made.

The second form of sex in the context of OBEs is when the subtle bodies of two people are drawn together sexually and they have intercourse in much the same way as it would be done on the physical level. Based on reports from people I have worked with over the years, it seems that this experience tends to take place in a more unconscious state, when those involved are operating on a more instinctual level. The experience includes the vividness of the OBE state and the recall of both people involved, but it does not include the full and conscious power of the third form of OBE sex.

The third form is often referred to as melding, because the experience has less to do with the usual sexual acts and more to do with an energetic exchange of essence and awareness. Melding is a truly profound experience and often leaves a deep telepathic and spiritual connection between people who experience it. Some readers may recognize this description from Tantra and sacred sexual practices. In this sense, melding takes place whenever there is a deep energetic and spiritual connection between people; it does not necessarily require leaving the body. Yet the experience reaches its fullest potential when it is done in this way. The mind feels like it is opening and one's awareness shifts to the other's perspective. Some people see themselves from the perspective of their lover; others reach an emotional link that reveals deep truths about their partner. "Sex" is a limiting term when applied to this kind of transformative interaction. It is, in fact, an opening of your identity, consciousness, and, in some cases, memories and deeply held unconscious aspects of yourself.

Sex beyond the body is best achieved with someone with whom you have a strong energetic bond. This is often easier to achieve when a relationship is fairly young and there is still a sense of what some refer to as "new relationship energy." This energy can draw both partners' consciousness or subtle bodies together, especially when you are physically separated. When trying to achieve this experience, I suggest spending some time together and learning some techniques from Western Tantra or sacred sexual practices, especially maintaining stimulation while holding off from the point of orgasm and focusing on the particular energy of your partner. Try to get in sync with their breathing, their movements, and even the subtle cues in their face. This can be a profound experience in itself. Slowing everything down to the point that you are barely moving will tune you to the other person in ways that you may not be aware of ordinarily. Gender and sexuality make no difference to this process; it is about engagement.

I advise going through this process for a week without reaching orgasm and then spend a few nights apart. On the first day, while you are alone, go through the same process without your partner; at the same time, he or she should do the same. Visualize them; try to experience everything they are experiencing until you feel an intense energy, almost like a tangible heat. Try to build this to the point that you experience a kind of sexual vibrational state. Once the sexual vibrational state is achieved, you will be able to leave your body and, if the connection was made with enough emotional investment, you should be drawn instantly to your partner. Once with him or her, you will likely be drawn into each other, filling each other and exchanging your full emotional depths.

A sexual connection in the form described above is another example of how out-of-body experiences can open us to a deeply transformative and spiritual realm in surprising and often unimagined ways. I feel that the potential for human interaction on this level has not been fully explored. This is partly due to the fact that achieving the necessary state is complex and requires a peak of emotional energy. It may also be due to the fact that other, more expansive levels of consciousness, such as contact with those who appear to have passed on, will sometimes present themselves. For most of us, this offers an amazing opportunity to explore the question of life after physical death.

Messages from the dead

Meetings with those who have physically died are often coloured by emotional confusion, as those who appear to have passed on are often confused, or in a slightly dreamlike state. There are many descriptions of this in literature on the afterlife and my own experiences seem to support this idea. We can never be totally sure, since these experiences are so subjective, yet extremely interesting "coincidences" have offered at least some degree of evidence that these experiences are valid and real. In one instance, I came upon a large group who seemed to have been killed in a plane crash, and a few hours after, I saw footage on the news of a similar accident. I didn't see any details in the experience to really make this connection concrete, but it suggests that there are ways to acquire some evidence, if only for your own benefit.

Early in my experiences, I seemed to connect more with those who were lingering on the physical plane in some form. Those writing about the more esoteric side of the OBE would claim that this is because at that time, when I was less developed, I was operating on a level similar to the one that spirits or ghosts inhabit. Whether or not this is the case I do not know, but I was able to communicate with individuals in the out-of-body state who gave particular details of their lives. In a few cases, I was able to find a record of a name matching the one I had heard in the OBE. There is always the possibility that I could have unconsciously picked up this information from another source, so I remain unsure of the exact nature of these early experiences. I was also very young at the time, and it is hard to say whether or not naivety could have played a role.

More compelling information has come in the form of images and experiences that seem similar to how some mediums describe the way they receive information. For example, two years ago I found myself out of my body and moving along the coastline of Cuba. I was at least 150 meters above the ground and able to see the whole layout of the surrounding areas as I moved. It was a beautiful and awe-inspiring sight. I felt so free and at peace as I drifted along, looking down at the rich colours and tropical waters. I remember small fisheries and the sense of people going about their lives. It was an almost utopian vision, and somehow that is what I think this experience represented. Shortly after the experience ended, I opened my diary to record the details and saw an entry about the death of a close family friend on the previous page. I had forgotten about writing this and during the experience I had not made the link to recent events. It dawned on me that the woman the entry was about was born in Cuba. She had been like family to me and had looked after me as a child when my mother was working. I now view this experience as a kind of message, reminding me that she is safe and at peace.

In my experiences with the transphysical levels, there is always a sense of distance between the living and the other levels. Their reality, while reachable and perceivable, is not a natural environment for us; it always seems a difficult journey to make. It reminds me of the myths and stories of those who would attempt to enter the underworld and the many trials and dangers they might face. These stories seem like metaphorical ways of emphasizing the distance between the worlds. It also seems as if the widespread shamanic worldview of the upper, middle, and underworlds reflects the out-of-body journeys of healers from across the globe. In many ways, the healers, mediums, and psychics that we have now are the shamans of our modern societies, framed in a media-driven world, yet somehow still appealing to the age-old needs and fears of humanity.

These modern shamanic practitioners also deal with our fears of the dark side of the spirit realm: our superstitions and belief in dark forces. The notion of negative beings is important—not because I believe that you will have anything to worry about, but because many people fear such things. Let's start by making it really clear: after many years and many hundreds of out-of-body experiences, I have *never* encountered anything harmful. I have also never had anything negatively affect my body or sense of well-being in any way whatsoever. There are those who believe in various forms of spirit possession and other types of negative influence, but if you take the view (as I do) that we are dealing with expansive interconnected consciousness, these ideas are soon revealed to be nothing more than a modern form of superstition. I sincerely hope that no one reading this book will be burdened with such ideas. However, if you do feel that your beliefs and fears may hold you back, you may find that working with some form of prayer, blessing, or affirmation before beginning might be helpful. You may also find it worthwhile to work in person at a workshop, or in a one-on-one session with a teacher, so you have support present. Others may find that calling upon some kind of protector, be it God or a spirit guide, is a useful means to feel more secure about leaving the body safely.

Spirit guides

Guides are one of the most amazing and at the same time puzzling aspects of both out-of-body and near-death experiences. They are found in narratives across cultures and in virtually all types of experience. Who or what these strange messengers are remains a mystery. Could they be an aspect of our unconscious, a form of collective consciousness, a human who has passed on, or a higher form of life? The answer to this is presently unclear, and may only ever be known on a personal, subjective level. But it seems clear that they are positive and often helpful in the actions and forms they take.

I have come across several accounts of people being helped out of their body by a being, or sometimes several beings. These beings would often become familiar to the person being guided, to the point that there would be an exchange of information and often advice being given. These descriptions go right back to the earliest works on the subject of OBEs and are still being described in current writing on the subject. For example, in the work of Rosalind McKnight, who learnt to have OBEs during the early days of Robert A. Monroe's research, the beings she encountered seemed to want to relate through her a whole array of information about the nature of life on Earth and our place in the scheme of the universe.

In my own experiences, too, I have found myself in several situations in which a being would offer guidance or suggest something to help me with circumstances in my life. One such incident took place on the transphysical level; I was in a level of reality that appeared full of yellow light, much like sunlight, but far more vivid and pervasive. I approached a figure that, though human in form, had a quality like he or she was only appearing in this form for my benefit. We sat communicating in some way, but while I was there the content of our communication seemed unimportant. I remember looking down at a river, also illuminated with golden light, and watching as other figures passed by, some with a full spectrum of colour flowing through them.

The being I was with smiled as I looked back, while looking deep into my eyes with a totally otherworldly quality, like I was fascinating to him in the same way a biologist might observe some intriguing detail of nature. The whole experience of being in the presence of this entity reminded me of another experience that took place during one of the few lucid dreams I've had. In the dream, I was having a reading from a kind of fortune-teller who was using a unique form of divination. She had the same quality as the being in the level of golden light described above. She looked deep into some part of me that I was not even totally aware of myself. When I awoke from the dream, I had the sense that I'd connected to something beyond normal reality and that the dream had simply been an access route for my awareness.

Even in my spiritual practice outside of the area of OBEs, I have encountered guides or what appear to be more advanced beings. Two of these came through to me while I was in deep trance, much like channeling, and seem to represent the essence of my spiritual understanding. They were called Shah and Mai, and those interested to learn about them can read more in my first book, *Avenues of the Human Spirit*. For the purposes of this book, I will simply say that they represented something akin to my higher self.

The whole idea of consciousness being extended does beg the question: Can other forms of consciousness impact or influence our awareness? It seems to me that this can be done to some degree, but the field of channeling seems complex; it would be extremely hard to differentiate between the unconscious mind of the person channeling and a separate entity or consciousness. However, just as the evidence supports telepathy and psi in general, I see no reason why we would not be capable of experiencing a full spectrum of consciousness. Maybe in the future new developments in science will open up yet more expansive and awe-inspiring levels of consciousness that we can't even imagine now.

10

ANOTHER REALITY:
MULTI-DIMENSIONAL
VISUALISATIONS

Back in the 1800s, a group of occultists in England founded the Hermetic Order of the Golden Dawn. Among their many rituals and beliefs was an approach called "traveling in the spirit vision." This was essentially a series of techniques designed to achieve a mild form of astral projection. Within this system, they used a group of images known as the tattva symbols, each of which was a simple shape, such as a square, a circle, a triangle, a crescent, and an egg, symbolizing earth, air, fire, water, and the aether, respectively, as well as combinations of each of them. The members of the Golden Dawn borrowed these designs from Hinduism, but adapted them to a different purpose. This system was later popularized in books on astral projection by modern writers such as J. H. Brennan, who wrote the foreword to this book.

The process involved the would-be traveler making a set of these colourful symbols on cardstock, which he or she would then use as an aid to meditation for an extended period of time, until the image became imprinted on the retina and the symbol seemed energised. The resulting negative image would seem to flash as your eyes adjusted. After a time, you were instructed to imagine the symbol beginning to grow until it was the size of a doorway. You would then allow the surface to dissolve in your mind's eye before shifting your awareness through the shape, so it acted like a portal.

Once on the other side, you would meet with a guide who would show you the nature and spiritual meaning of that particular symbol. As in other guided meditation systems, you often gain a piece of information or guidance that has particular importance to you, either spiritually or in a magical sense. Once you reached the point at which you felt you had seen enough, or the energy was drawing you back, you were supposed to retrace your journey exactly until you passed back through the portal and closed it behind you. You would then go through the whole process in reverse until you felt comfortable and grounded again. The result of these journeys through the tattvas was often very powerful and could be compared to mild OBEs, in some cases.

A Tattva Vision

One of my first tattva experiments with the fire triangle, Tajas, felt like an extremely vivid waking dream. I remember lighting a candle and sitting cross-legged on the floor, holding a small card onto which I had painted the red triangle. I sat staring intently at the surface. At first, the texture of the paint and the canvas-like card distracted me from focusing completely on the symbol, but after a while the triangle began to almost burn into my eyes. I slowly let my eyes close and my hands drop into my lap as the red of the triangle began to pulse and shift in my mind, as if it was somehow conscious and reacting to my internal dialogue. I focused again, this time with the intention of bringing the image into line and not losing the purpose of the exercise. The image seemed to become a dark bluish tone, the negative of its original red, and began to grow in size.

Soon the shape seemed to take up my whole awareness and floated just a few feet in front of me like a grand painting. Yet the surface was not fixed and static; it became shadowy and vague, like there was something in the distance obscured by mist. In an attempt to see what was there, I shifted my awareness forward and in an instant I felt myself falling through space. I found myself in an open, natural environment with trees and colourful flowers all around. The grass seemed to have a golden hue to it, like an aura highlighting its outline, and the sky faded from turquoise to rich shades of mauve and pink.

As I stood there taking in the sheer beauty of the scene, a figure began to approach from the horizon. He seemed otherworldly to me as he stopped a few feet away. His eyes didn't seem to have the expression and empathy that we expect from a human being, and his clothing and appearance in general was slightly fantastical, with rich patterns and unusual forms. Looking at him, I remembered that the tattva instructions also recommended a test, a way of finding out if this part of the universe or aspect of my unconscious was truly a guide and benevolent or something more sinister. I traced a symbol in the air as the book I was reading had advised me and waited to see how he would react. At first nothing, so I continued to focus on positive, life-giving energy, before directing it straight at him. At this point he grew and expanded with the energy. It was clear that, far from harming him, it was transforming him, showing clearly that he was a guide, just as the book described.

At that he turned and, gesturing with his strange blank eyes, we began to walk. I seemed to be able to move with a new freedom and lightness, like I was being helped, and even lifted slightly from the ground. The scenery too seemed to reflect my guide's changed nature, and all around creative new forms of life and colour began to appear. As we moved, I also felt like some kind of knowledge was being transferred to me, as well as the ability to draw from reserves of creative energy that I didn't know I had.

Finally, after what seemed like an unknowable, timeless period, this strange being turned and indicated that we should return the way we had come. As we did so, it was as if everything that we had seen or disturbed on our way to that point was also rolling back, returning to its original state before I had come here. All the life seemed to morph and change as we passed, like it was returning to a state of pure energy. Finally we were back where we had met, at which point I turned to offer some kind of thanks, only to discover that he had vanished, along with much of the scene that was now becoming little more than a shadow again. Moments later, I felt my awareness drifting back to myself and my sense of the room and the flickering candle returning.

Three-Dimensional Tattvas

When I started studying the various methods of astral projection in my teens, tattva system experiences like the above had a strong impact on me. However, they didn't seem to initiate a full out-of-body experience; there seemed to be something missing. In the late 1990s, the idea dawned on me that these astral doorways only operate on a two-dimensional level—they are simply flat images. What was needed was something that would impact the mind and the unconscious with a full three-dimensional approach. I had no idea at the time how much potential this would have and how many other areas it would open up.

Tajas, the fire triangle, had been the most powerful in my personal experiments, so I decided to work with the idea of making it three-dimensional. Obviously this would result in a pyramid, a shape that is already loaded with symbolic meaning and a whole range of beliefs dating back millennia. I experimented with ways I could work with the pyramidal structure to create the best results. Then, in a visualisation experiment in which I pictured two triangles in front of me, I noticed a very interesting and unexpected element to this way of working. The energies from the first tattva doorway seemed to influence those from the second. As I focused on them, this effect seemed to increase. First, a blending of energy or influence and meaning took place, then a new portal or doorway seemed to form from the combination of the first two. This had radical implications: there was a growth process going on, almost like the shapes mimicking nature and reproducing themselves to create new and unimagined energies or forms. I discovered that the more complex the shape, the more complex and fascinating the resulting energy and psychological impact would be.

The pyramid

This opened up amazing possibilities. What would happen when I added additional tattvas and formed the full pyramid? Whether this was just a psychological impact of the complex visualisation, or something operating on another level, wasn't the key element. An energetic foundation was being formed that would lead to more powerful experiences. As I added the other sides of the pyramid in my visualisation, the effect did indeed magnify. Each side seemed to have a new and fascinating impact on the previous sides. Once all the sides were "open," I was surrounded by an energy that seemed to be enhancing itself exponentially, drawing me into the experience. The result was an energy of a totally new order to any I'd experienced before. I felt renewed by it, even rebuilt.

When I first taught this new approach to others, I noticed that it had a powerful impact on them as well. The first time was at a meeting in the open air in an area of South London. We made our way up the hill to a clearing surrounded by trees that would serve well for this kind of work. We all took up our positions in a small circle and, after a basic introduction to the process, I began to guide the group through the visualisation. I kept the description as simple as I could, vividly describing the formation of one triangle at a time. I waited until the image was clear and radiating in my mind before moving to the next step. I looked deep into the triangular form and began to see the surface dissolving away until a sense of a landscape, location, or energy form became apparent.

The first triangle already seemed to have an amazingly healing and powerful feeling about it. I felt anticipation at the prospect of looking into the second and subsequent shapes. As soon as I sensed everyone was ready, I began to describe the second triangle. Now, as its surface began to dissolve, I sensed a pure energy, and with each subsequent doorway, this clearer, more crystalline feeling continued to grow. The energies from the first and second triangles seemed to blend and enhance each other in ways that I could never have predicted. It was a blend of healing, sensation, and the many emotions of life, from inspiration to love to joy. I felt a stream of light and connection running through my body, from my feet straight up through the top of my head. I had not felt anything comparable since an OBE in which I felt I was at one with all the minds in the universe.

With each subsequent triangle, a new movement and particular interaction was taking place, until finally they formed a whole, a pyramid, and I was drawn into its swirling energy. It felt like being drawn into a whirlpool of light and pure force. A moment later, I felt like I was several feet away from the group, looking back at myself standing rooted to the spot. It was more like being in two places at once than a standard out-of-body experience, and I was still able to guide the others as we began to reverse the process and go back, carefully shutting each doorway the way we had opened it.

Afterward, we all felt rooted by an energy that seemed to be coming right up through the earth. We all took quite a while to properly ground ourselves and "close down." We spent a further few minutes discussing how we felt before beginning the short journey down the hill toward the road. It was clear, as I looked out across London as I descended, that I'd found a way of working with human psychology and whatever energy or interconnectedness might exist that would have almost limitless potential.

The process did not end with the pyramid form. I began to explore other structures, such as the cube and the sphere. If you take a moment to think about it, the sphere is a three-dimensional form but also has no sides as such. This makes it the most powerful shape in many ways to use as a visualisation or meditational aid. It seems that the more challenging the form of the visualisation, the more it can impact us in a way that stretches and pushes our mental skills (see page 189 for a technique based on the pyramid).

The sphere

There are many connections between the sphere and the transphysical level. Many, including myself, have experienced what appeared to be spirits in the form of orbs or spheres. The chakras have been described as spinning wheels of energy within the body. In Dante's classic poetic work *The Divine Comedy*, we see the other world ordered like spheres within spheres. Some scientists even envision a multi-verse of spherical universes like bubbles rising to the surface of a vast lakelike meta-universe. All of these notions fit well with the sphere visualisation that I have developed (see page 189).

The real power of the sphere is the fact that it is the only form or shape that has only one side, no beginning, and no end; thus the approach that I took with the pyramid and other shapes becomes redundant when applied to the sphere. It took me a lot of practice envisioning a sphere in my mind to get the idea of this single-surfaced form opening on itself, much like the other shapes in the multi-dimensional system, but once I did, I found that a whole new level of energy and mental agility was achieved. It may take you weeks or even months to be able to hold the idea of the sphere opening its whole form like a doorway, but once you can do this, you will be able to take this method to the next level.

Once you have become confident working with a single sphere, try bringing in a second, much as you did when adding a second triangle to the pyramid—only this time see what happens when you overlap them. Does this change the way they feel? Or impact the way the energy acts? The next step is to overlap them until they blend together. What happens as they totally envelop each other? If at any point you notice them vibrating, pulsing, or undulating like a wave, try moving them close to you. Does this impact your body? If this feels comfortable, move the sphere into your body, and move the energy up into your head and out again, if you wish. If you notice the vibrational state beginning to take hold, go with it. Try to focus on it and build the sensations until the line between your physical body and the energy becomes blurred.

———————————

As you can see, the sphere or pyramid visualisations can be excellent ways of bringing about the high vibrational sensations that often suggest an out-of-body experience is close. I recommend experimenting with different shapes and approaches to see which works best for you. As I've pointed out throughout this book, there is no one approach that will work with everyone. Look at the profile you developed in Chapter 4, and also the fears and strengths that you have identified, and take these into account. All of us have limits and boundaries; it is just part of being human—no one is perfect. The best approach is to find the most powerful ways to work within your limits, so that they become strengths and avenues to success in any particular endeavour.

You may well find with time that you can induce the vibrational state without the need to use processes such as these three-dimensional visualisation techniques. I have learnt to sense when an OBE is close. Sometimes I can sense the vibrational state even before I have relaxed. The particular feeling that comes with the state simply becomes apparent. This has wider implications than just the out-of-body state: it suggests that this energy is available for other purposes.

Geometric Patterns and Consciousness

Around the same time that I began exploring the tattva system within my OBE training, I also began to work with yantras, or geometric patterns believed to have a spiritual meaning. As well as having an inherent power within the Hindu tradition, they are also used as a focus within meditation. This interested me, being an artistic and very visual person, because I had come across virtually no other form of meditation that could explore colour, form, and geometry in this way. I remember the Shri Yantra in particular seemed to have a powerful impact on my consciousness. I would enter a state that felt much like a flowering of awareness was taking place. The longer I focused on the symbol, the more it would reveal itself to me and I would find myself flowing down tunnels of immense beauty. It was like the mathematical structure of life was being revealed. I remember watching an animation of the Mandelbrot Set (a fractal that has some startling similarities to the forms and structures found in nature) and feeling that on some level the Shri Yantra was revealing a similar fractal-like nature to me.

As my meditation practice grew, I began to find that even when I was doing simple meditations, I would often begin to see complex geometric forms. During one meditation session with a partner, I began to see two overlapping triangles at the height of the experience, before they joined to become a unicursal hexagram. At the time, I had never seen a hexagram that was joined in the center, as is the case with a unicursal hexagram, so I was fascinated. I became more fascinated when I eventually came across a diagram by Aleister Crowley that matched what I had seen. I became interested in Crowley's work for a time, although his rather negative image had put me off of engaging with him until that point. However, I ultimately returned to my original conclusion that, while brilliant and in many ways a revolutionary thinker, Crowley was largely misguided and the product of his puritanical upbringing.

Yet the power of geometric forms still fascinated me. After all, the multi-dimensional approach aligns well with the notion that the nearest levels of reality to the physical level may be geometric in nature, or that consciousness is like an array of information spread out as a kind of network. This also relates well to the idea of cosmic consciousness, but goes further since some writers believe that entities or beings on other levels of reality may be perceived by us as a geometric structure. Much like the other ideas discussed in this chapter, this is a purely subjective possibility and should only be looked at in that context. However, many scientists including Isaac Newton believed in a kind of alchemical nature to the universe, in which symbols and mathematical forms have a greater significance than the purely intellectual. In religions, too, we find the complex geometry present in Islamic temples, the amazing art of the Tibetan Buddhist mandalas, the stained glass of Christian churches, and the ancient structures of Britain such as Stonehenge and Avebury, the largest stone circle in the world and a complex design of circles within circles. We are naturally drawn to the belief that complex shapes and patterns can impact our lives in a direct way.

The work of Masaru Emoto suggests that there may be some relationship between consciousness and harmonious or geometric forms. Emoto has conducted experiments on water to see whether prayer, intention, or meditational focus would change the form of crystals in water once it was frozen. The photographs that he has produced seem to clearly show that an effect is produced. At present, this is a controversial idea, and I remain neutral as to whether this is the case. However, in 2006 Dean Radin achieved positive results in his first replication of Emoto's work, stating, "Results indicated that crystals from the treated water were given higher scores for aesthetic appeal than those from the control water (p=0.001, one-tailed), lending support to the hypothesis."[1] In 2009, Radin again gained positive results in a triple-blind experiment using some 2,500 independent judges.[2]

The relationships between geometric and three-dimensional forms and consciousness, healing, and even the very structure of water molecules have yet to be fully unraveled, but are full of fascinating possibilities. While these areas remain conjecture at this point in time, the connection between consciousness and matter becomes stronger with each new area of enquiry. Take the now-famous "observer effect," which says that the more we look into the basis of reality, the more we find that what we understand as "real" only assumes a particular form when we observe or measure it. While this is a somewhat controversial area (and I don't for a moment claim to have any advanced understanding of physics), it is clear that this has huge implications for anyone interested in consciousness and whether we can transcend the limitations of our body and even gain some fundamental understanding of the universal questions.

When I had my first out-of-body experiences, the concept of matter being fluid and intimately linked to our conscious awareness was natural to me. I had no need of science to convince me; I could look deep into matter with nonphysical eyes and see complex patterns of life swirling back at me. While I understood little of what I saw, I sense looking back that—like the religious visionaries, shamans, and mystics before me—I had an intuitive understanding of what was happening. That in the end I would reach a point where I would understand that everything is one, and I would essentially come full circle. And that is what I think has happened on a fundamental level. I now fully embrace the limitations of what I can know and experience, because that also teaches me what I can experience and reminds me how important the journey really is.

HEALING AND
THE OUT-OF-BODY
EXPERIENCE

The ability of the mind to heal the body through the power of one's belief has long been a topic of study. Doctors and researchers are in a constant battle, when developing new medicines and approaches, to overcome the mysterious placebo effect. When someone is given a placebo drug, or a placebo treatment they *believe* to be effective, the result can sometimes be as effective as the real drug or the real treatment, even though in reality the pills are little more than sugar pills. What does this mean? In simple terms, it means that the consciousness or mind of the individual has directly shaped the healing processes within his or her body. This further implies that consciousness can change the potential outcome of that person's reality. Some consider this a radical notion, but when we introduce the ideas that consciousness is not limited to the body, and that even the nature of our world may be much more fluid and far less objective than it appears on the surface, the possibility becomes more intriguing.

In mainstream medicine, the placebo effect is the reason that much of complementary or alternative medicine is dismissed. Although many alternative healing approaches seem to perform little better than would be expected as a result of strong belief in the treatment, there are also many documented instances of a radical turnaround in the health of some individuals undergoing therapies such as acupuncture or energy healing. It seems to me that, much like premonitions and other psi phenomena as discussed earlier, these states of enhanced healing take place at peak moments. They are not, and indeed cannot be, everyday occurrences any more than an athlete could match his or her personal best at each performance.

Once we begin to look at things in this way, the issue then becomes: how can we reach a state of heightened or peak healing? Could experiences of altered consciousness, such as the out-of-body state, help us do it more effectively? It is still early to say whether the vibrational state or the out-of-body experience could be utilised as effective healing methods, but there are many reasons to suppose they could be.

Healing Energies

The type of energy experienced both in the vibrational state and in the full OBE has a lot in common with healing energies. Of course, we don't really know what these so-called energies are, or even if they are actual energies at all, but out-of-body experiences seem to have a beneficial impact on the body and that energy is often a part of that process (at least in an experiential sense).

The well-known healing system, Reiki, gives us a clue as to the nature of this energy. The word "Reiki" derives from Japanese but uses kanji, which are characters of Chinese origin. If we break the word into its two parts, *rei* essentially means "spirit," while *ki* means "energy." When we fully understand Reiki as spiritual energy, it's easier to see how leaving the physical body for healing purposes is a direct way of experiencing spiritual or nonphysical energy.

Robert A. Monroe, for example, believed that leaving the body was a part of the body's natural process of maintaining health and well-being. He believed that we go through some kind of out-of-body shift as we sleep. In a 1979 interview, he explained the process as he saw it: "During what we call delta sleep at night, which everyone goes through, is quite probably, according to our researches, a time when everybody goes into this out-of-body state. You don't remember it, but it does take place...It is somewhat the recharging mechanism that you get during sleep."[1]

Monroe was not alone in the belief that the OBE is a part of the natural process of recharging during sleep. Sylvan Muldoon and Hereward Carrington, authors of *Projection of the Astral Body,* believed that the purpose of sleep was connected to the subtle body or a vital energy. Carrington wrote: "We shall never arrive at a satisfactory theory of sleep, doubtless, until we admit the presence of a vital force and the existence of an individual human spirit, which withdraws more or less completely from the body during the hours of sleep, and derives spiritual invigoration and nourishment during its sojourn in the spiritual world."[2] While none of these statements go very far to explain how this process might work, there is a consensus that the out-of-body experience contains a revitalizing aspect.

Like these authors, I also believe that something important related to our health and well-being is taking place. When I lift out of my body, I often feel an enormous release, like tensions and blocks are being cleared away. It feels in some ways like going for a run on a brisk day—the pressures of every-day life are quickly swept away by the wind in your face, leaving you feeling alive and clear when you return home. Many spiritual experiences have this kind of effect on us; they leave us feeling peaceful, vital, and connected.

In a conversation with Dr. Peter Fenwick, a physician and expert on the impact of transcendent states, I asked about his views on consciousness and spiritual healing. He said, "There is no doubt there is such a thing as spiritual healing. There are processes there that are entanglement processes, that are different from straight immune system function." He also explained that he thought sometimes the catalyst of a physical action, such as laying hands on the body, or holding them over it, is useful and that spiritual healing is far more than simply a placebo. He continued that he believes the process may be linked to a transcendent reality or a kind of conscious universe.[3]

At present, though, the scientific evidence for spiritual healing is still thin. This does not mean that healing in this form is untrue; it simply means that little research has been done, or what research that does exist is inconsistent. This is why supporting alternative areas of research in science is so important. If there is a benefit to energetic healing, and the ability to heal is latent in human beings, not investigating the possibility fully would be a disaster to our spirit of inquiry, as well as our humanity.

My Experiences with Healing Others

In the early days of my OBEs, I attempted healing via the OBE state, not because I particularly associated this state with healing at the time, but because I wondered if there was a relationship. I believe that those around me may have also wondered if this special experience could have some benefit to those in need of healing. I remember at school a friend requesting my help. I recall the way I could directly feel the vibrations of the other person and, if required, lift their energy in such a way that, to my perception, their vibration would begin to match mine. This seems to have the effect over time of helping to heal the person involved.

In the specific experience with a sick teenager from my school, whom my friend asked me to help, I wasn't sure what the result would be. I lay down on my bed at the other side of the city and began to focus in on the person. Almost as soon as I did, I felt my intention to help bringing on the vibrational state. My body pulsed with yellowish-golden light. I held the experience of connecting deeply with the energy and the feelings flowing through me, before releasing myself to the experience and lifting out of my body. I found myself up above some unknown part of London before I focused in on the teenager again. Within moments I was next to her bed, sensing her illness and her lack of energy. She appeared quite gray and without any real sign of the energy of life. I drew upon all of my willpower in an attempt to raise her energy and bring her closer to the vital state that I was in. She responded by moving and seeming to take on the energy I was cultivating within her body. When I left her that night, she had a steady flow of energy much like the vibrational state.

It is hard to know how objective these perceptions were, but I was told by her friend that her health improved markedly, so much so that her doctor had made a note of it and remarked that this was very unusual. I also learnt that she had no awareness of any of this. To avoid what we would now call the placebo effect, her friend had not told her about the healing attempt beforehand or visited her on the night in question.

This was in fact my first experiment with healing in any form. It was some years later before I would explore the possibility again, during a trip to a sacred site called Avebury in southern England. A friend called Euca asked me to do some healing work on him. It was close to the harvest festival of Lammas and there was quite a gathering of people all around the area, despite the fact that it was already dark. It was hard to find a place away from people where we could concentrate. We decided to stand next to the two largest of the standing stones that surround the small village, as most people had gathered on the bank to watch the large full moon rising. We stood in front of the stone and I began turning my awareness inward and specifically began to focus on the vibrational state. I soon perceived a darkened area near Euca's shoulder. I asked if he had any issues with his shoulder, to which he answered that he was slightly shocked at me picking this up, but yes, he had been experiencing problems with it for some time.

I seemed to sense the subtler energies running through him; whether this was really the case or not, I don't know, but it seemed at the very least a psychological representation of what was taking place on a psychic level. I began to notice what seemed like fibers or strings of energy becoming disentangled and the darkened area began to change and harmonise with the rest of his energy.

When I returned home afterward, I noticed that the heightened energy I had experienced felt closely aligned to the vibrational state that I would often experience shortly before an OBE. I think that night, and the thoughts that came to me after, formed the early stages of a new understanding of healing.

Somehow, the connection between OBEs and healing has been all but overlooked, probably because it is actually so obvious that it's hard to grasp. I wonder if healing might actually be a form of psi phenomena, much like psychokinesis acting on an illness. Or maybe it's not so much about energy fields or the way we view energy, but more about consciousness interacting with others, or maybe the world. This combination of subtle physiological and psychical awareness may well be how healing actually works.

Of course, modern scientifically based medicine should never be denied or overlooked. The forms of healing I'm exploring are complementary to modern medicine, not a replacement for it. This is a really important point, since many people fear the actions of science when it comes to medicine. The best thing you can do to allay these fears is to become familiar with the research being done.

All of these things seem to point toward reality, energy, and consciousness being linked in some complex way, so that psychological changes can lead to a change in the way we experience the world.

Practical Vibrational State Healing

The best approach you can use related to alternative healing methods is to try some exercises for yourself and see what results you get. Generally, there is good evidence that if you believe in what you are doing, you will get some positive results. This particularly applies to experimenting with the out-of-body state.

There are two concepts to be aware of in using the out-of-body state for healing. The first is to understand that the condition or illness that you are working with is just one potential state of being. Those potentials, it appears, can be changed or shifted; thus no outcome is set in stone. The second factor concerns the experiential aspect of the out-of-body state. The state is like an energy field that contains a kind of blueprint, which you might call your second body, subtle body, or extended consciousness. But what is important is that this sense of yourself beyond the body does not contain the limitations, acquired fears and beliefs, or learnt behaviors that you have developed during your lifetime.

When you bear these two factors in mind, you realise that within the OBE, the healing process is related to directly experiencing this more genuine aspect of ourselves. Like the mindfulness experienced during meditation, being in the out-of-body state connects us to our unfettered self, which in turn promotes well-being and healing.

EXERCISE: SHARING ENERGY WITH A PARTNER

- Step 1: In the first part of this exercise, you will need to develop the vibrational state, or at least a level of awareness closely related to the early stages of an OBE (since, as discussed, not everyone experiences the full vibrational state). The goal here is not to fully leave body awareness, but to increase your sensation of subtle shifts and flows in consciousness as much as possible. You will find the Three-Dimensional Doorway Technique (see page 187) helpful with this, as well as the Bellows Breath Technique (see page 202).

- Step 2: I suggest sitting in a simple crossed-legged posture with your partner lying flat in front of you. Instruct your partner to focus on your breathing to start with, and any sense of the flow of your energy he or she might become aware of. Your partner should continue to focus on your energy throughout the exercise.

- Step 3: Once you feel the level of energy in your body at its height—especially if you feel a wavelike sensation or vibrations—start to expand the motion of the waves or vibrations outward. Concentrate on the boundary or edge of the sensations and push outward a little—not too far, just enough to begin to push the energy out toward your partner.

- Step 4: Once the energy is radiating outwardly, toward your partner, extend your arms out, palms down, and start to concentrate the sense of energy within and around your hands. Sense the flow of the vibrational state all around your body and out over the body of your partner.

- Step 5: Now start to shift your awareness to the position of your partner, as if you are starting to have an OBE. Let your awareness move around his or her body seeking places where the energy feels blocked in some form. This may feel like a resistance, or like tangled fibers. Sense what part of the body the blockage is in and begin to concentrate your awareness there, bringing the vibrations over this part of the body. You might also want to move your hands to this area of your partner's body.

- Step 6: Place your awareness as fully as you can into the vibrational field and sense the blockage beginning to match the heightened frequency of your vibrational state. Continue until the blockage is no longer apparent.

- Step 7: At this point, try to activate the vibrational state in your partner. He or she should still be focused on your energy as instructed in step 1. Start to picture in your mind the conscious awareness of your partner and try to infuse that image with the vibrational energy all around you. Try to draw your partner into sync with you.

· Step 8: Hold this mutual state for as long as feels comfortable. When you're ready to finish, place your hands on the ground and let the vibrational energy subside naturally. It may help to imagine the energy flowing into the ground as a way of returning yourself to normal everyday consciousness.

After completing this exercise, you may want to discuss it and get feedback from your partner about what he or she experienced. I advise writing this down in your journal, and seeing whether or not your perceptions were correct. As with any methodology, it may take some practice to get a good sense of what is happening with your own energy, and how it interacts with the energy of the other person.

———————————

The out-of-body experience can have a powerful impact on the personal well-being of the individual. It can lead to a total change in values, and even lifestyle. As our awareness of both the out-of-body state and our inner ability to heal and maintain optimum health continues to grow, I expect the OBE to become a more widely accepted aspect of the spectrum of complementary methods for living a more spiritual, harmonious, and holistic life. I sincerely hope that there will be more scientific research into this important field.

All areas of psychic and spiritual understanding hold fascinating possibilities and clues to our innermost nature. They challenge us and open our perceptions to ways of looking at the world we hadn't imagined before. In the next chapter, we will explore one of the most challenging psychic abilities I have personally encountered—the ability to perceive forward or backward through time.

12

CERULEAN DAWN: PERCEIVING ACROSS TIME

The out-of-body experience holds the potential for us to move our awareness to any point in the universe, but it can also allow us to travel beyond the limits of time—a possibility that has both challenged and fascinated me since my first experiences. Many explorers of consciousness have found that time and space seem fluid, malleable, or even totally illusory. For example, Joseph McMoneagle, the famous remote viewer who developed his skills as part of the U.S. military's secret Stargate program, found that time was no more of an obstacle than any other. In fact, many in the world of parapsychology, as well as some physicists, now believe that the future can influence the past. This notion is called reverse causality or retrocausality and, if true, could change the way in which we understand *everything*.

Precognition in Action

Dean Radin at the Institute of Noetic Sciences in California has demonstrated an unconscious awareness of the future in volunteers. These presentiment experiments show that shortly before an emotional image is shown to an individual, they will react on an unconscious level as if they have already seen the image.[1] The response is generally measured by monitoring electrical activity in the skin of the volunteers, much like the process used for biofeedback devices. Again, the implications are huge; it implies that we may have an innate awareness, although largely unconscious, of events before they happen. Some have suggested that this represents an ancient survival mechanism, which would give us a subtle early warning when danger is near. Psychic abilities in this sense would offer an evolutionary advantage in hostile predatory environments such as the Earth of the past.

My experiences with precognition: The Soho bombing

This idea of an early warning fits in well with common descriptions of premonitions and/or a sense of foreboding shortly before a major disaster, and is something I have experienced in my own life. My understanding of how time and space work was challenged for the first time when I found myself beyond my body, standing on the corner of Moor Street and Old Compton Street in central London. The scene was powerful and vivid, despite the fact that my vision was infused with a grayish-blue or cerulean light that seemed to have a unique energetic quality. (I had only ever experienced this cerulean-blue vision once before, and that had been one of the most objectively verifiable of all my out-of-body experiences.)

I felt fixed to the spot, not in the sense of not being able to move—I feel I could have if I had tried—but rather that I knew instinctively that staying where I was was the right thing to do. As I stood there motionless, an explosion burst out of a building in the distance, on the right of the main road. Almost immediately, a man ran past me, heading for the site of the explosion. I watched as the scene changed from calm everyday life in Soho to anguish and disbelief. I felt a wave of emotion and sensed that this was not an accident; it was an extremely important event that had yet to take place.

Five days later, a bombing took place, just as I had seen in my OBE. This was obviously very hard to fully grasp; had I actually seen a future event, or was this simply a coincidence? At first I didn't know what to believe. I always maintain a level of healthy skepticism when faced with such experiences, but I couldn't ignore the high level of accuracy.

My experiences with precognition: The 7/7 attacks

A few years later, my sense of what was possible was challenged again. This time I found myself floating above Moorgate Underground Station in the city of London, my vision again tinted with cerulean blue. Within moments I was following a train as it clashed and rattled along the line into Liverpool Street Station, one stop down the line. I remember pausing at the back of the train as it pulled away from Liverpool Street and headed for Aldgate East. Then came a wave of emotion and anguish that seemed to be rolled into the shockwave of an explosion up ahead. Again, it was obvious that I was witnessing a terrorist attack, and again I believed it would take place at some point in the future.

Since I was more aware than I had been during my experience with the Soho attack, I decided to try and gain some sense of when this latest event might take place. Unfortunately I could only pick up glimpses of the numerals 5 or 05. This experience took place some time in April 2004, so I took this to mean May, the following month, or 2005, the following year. This was far from the precision I had hoped for, but this level of detail is simply the way that the information comes through. Gaining details from these experiences is something like walking through a room once and then trying to describe all the details some time after.

Moments later, I was back in the apartment I was living in at the time. This experience impacted my life for the next year, until the event did take place as I'd seen it, on July 7, 2005. I avoided the underground stations in that part of London, and I had a general feeling of compassion towards all those who would become involved.

Experiments with Time

It was clear that I could not simply dismiss these experiences as coincidence. I began researching precognition as well as talking to people such as Dean Radin about their views. I also read anything I could find that gave some scientific context to the experience. One such book was J. W. Dunne's *An Experiment with Time*, in which he explains that precognition is common, especially in dream states. He outlines a system for observing your dreams and comparing them to events in waking reality. The result, he claims, is that many dreams appear to be precognitive in nature. Rupert Sheldrake, the British scientist whose work I discussed earlier, states in his book *The Sense of Being Stared At* that he was able to experience similar precognitive perceptions by recording his dreams in the way that Dunne suggests.

Sheldrake also believes that consciousness operates through a form of causation from the future to the past. This involves the concept that consciousness is operating on the level of potentialities, also discussed earlier. Physical reality meets with this level of consciousness in the present. He believes that, on a quantum level, this would be referred to as the collapse of the wave function, which means a single possibility becomes an actual occurrence *after* the involvement of an observer. I was actually able to use this understanding to get the highest score ever in a single trial on a computer-controlled, random precognition test designed by Sheldrake; whether this is repeatable to any degree remains to be seen. While a single trial in any area is not conclusive, it does at least suggest that the future influencing the past may have some truth to it. This is also another example of how an awareness of current scientific theories may help us optimise our psychic functioning.

As research in these areas becomes more computer-controlled and more people gain access to psi testing via the Internet, the evidence will become the best it can be; human error will be almost removed from the argument, as will claims of cheating. The only downside that may arise with scientific trials of telepathy, precognition, and remote viewing going online is an overly casual attitude toward the tests. In some online trials, there is already a tendency for some participants to abandon the test before they have completed it, which then stands as a negative trial and brings down the average results. Two possible solutions would be to include an incentive to finish the trial, or to make the process of joining a test harder, so that only those with a genuine wish to take part will take the time to complete the process.

If we do continue to find evidence for precognition in a scientific way, we will be entering a fascinating period in history when consciousness really does become the ultimate unexplored territory. You have probably heard the dictum that we know more about the vastness of space than we do about the oceans of our world. Maybe, with the help of radical scientists willing to explore and question, we will turn our attention even closer to home and explore the true nature of the mind and human consciousness.

An Historical Approach to Precognition

The idea that human beings can perceive events before they occur is a very old and persistent one. Names such as Nostradamus have entered the popular imagination and new prophets and prophecies arise in every generation. I remember as a small boy visiting the home of Mother Shipton, a seer who is thought to have predicted the Great Fire of London in 1666. The magic of the cave and the well inspired my imagination, and I still own the small booklet of her predictions that my parents bought me during that visit. To my mother and father, the tales of figures like Shipton were and are simply a bit of fun; as for me, I wondered if there might be a clue in some part of her writings as to the nature of my own unusual experiences.

Going even further back into history, we have the stories of the Oracle at Delphi, a woman believed to be in communication with Apollo, the Sun

God. Interestingly, there seems to be some crossover between the methods of these ancient prophets and figures like Nostradamus. In Delphi, the Oracle was said to sit on top of a tripod and gaze into the surface of water. Nostradamus also used a tripod and a form of reaching into trance to see the future called scrying. This is the same process used with a crystal ball, or the surface of water, or a mirror for the purpose of having visions of the future or to gain information, not dissimilar to the modern process of remote viewing. Even John Dee, an English mathematician and advisor to Queen Elizabeth I, used scrying with the help of a seer by the name of Edward Kelley, although Dee and Kelley did not generally focus on seeing the future. Scrying continues to be used by psychics and spiritual seekers today.

After learning about scrying, I tried using a range of materials to see if I could uncover any benefits to this approach. I tried using water, crystal, ink, and even smoke as a medium through which to perceive psychically. But it turned out that a black mirror, somewhat like the one that is now on display in the British Museum once belonging to Dee, was most effective in my experience.

To begin, I would sit in a comfortable position in front of a round sheet of glass that I had spray-painted on the reverse to give an even black surface. I would usually do this in candlelight and sometimes with incense. After a time of staring at the surface, my mind would seem to drift into the blackness, like looking into a starless sky. I would find that images would arise, forms and shapes followed by identifiable scenes and people. However, I only ever experienced a few things that could be categorised as precognitive, for example, seeing someone in the mirror I had not seen for some time, only to bump into that person a few hours later. In other words, little mundane glimpses of what may or may not have been future events. Overall, scrying is an excellent way to train your perceptions, so for that alone it is worthwhile, and, depending on the person, may also help to open precognitive awareness for those interested in explore this area further.

Seeing into the Past

While the future has always fascinated us, there is also a long tradition of belief in seeing the past. The akashic records, seen as a kind of store or library of the entire knowledge and experience of the world (and maybe of all worlds), feature highly in many writers' descriptions of the astral planes, and are believed by some to provide a way to access the past.

While I don't take on the esoteric beliefs surrounding ideas like the akashic records, I find that my own experiences seeing past events through the OBE do resemble in many ways a recording. I remember one occurrence when I floated out of the apartment I was living in at the time to find myself not in the modern-day street outside but instead in what appeared to be a Victorian version of it. I drifted across the large London road that would usually be full of cars and buses, passing by horses, black carriages with a brownish dirty appearance, and carts roughly cobbled together from wood and coated with thick, colourful paint. Yet apart from the buildings that lined the immediate road around me and what looked like a small church, the scene was bare, with the area from which I had just come looking green and open, far from how this part of London looks in the modern day. I remember watching grand-looking gentlemen dressed in top hats and groomed to a degree that seemed unusual to my eyes. Flowing through the streets around them, operating on a totally different tempo, were men and women of a different class. They seemed to have an urgency about them, as if they needed to be somewhere and if they weren't, there would be extreme consequences. The whole scene felt like two worlds (actually two social classes) operating without awareness of each other.

As I moved farther along the street, I began to notice a familiar building or turn in the road. The houses, though far from the twenty-floor apartment blocks that now stand in the area, did seem somehow like a place I had been before, in my own time. Their gray and brownish stone facades seemed to connect me back to the time from which I had come. It was all the more intriguing to follow this route toward the center of the city, as I had done so many times before, both physically and in OBEs. In fact, moving along this road had become a routine way of getting to other parts of the city when I was out of my body, so much so that I was familiar with many small details along the route. Yet now only a vague impression of what might one day become the everyday was present.

As I began to feel more comfortable and the experience seemed at its peak, I felt the familiar sense that I was being drawn back to normal consciousness, back to my body. I tried to push in the opposite direction, to hold on a little longer so I could retain a little more of what I was seeing, but it was impossible. I was already reaching my body and my awareness was shifting back to the familiar details of my bedroom.

While this experience had many of the elements I would normally expect when out of the body, somehow it was very different. I wonder whether it was some kind of past-life memory or energetic memory recorded in the very stone of this place, or if it was actually a journey to the akashic records. Whatever it was, it didn't seem like an experience with a living consciousness. Although I cannot physically interact with people I might encounter in an OBE, there is usually a sense that they might potentially become aware of me and that the events are taking place at the same moment the people are in. In other words, they are in the same time awareness as I am. In this particular experience, I did not get the sense that the people I saw were present in the same time awareness as me, or even that they were aware on another level. I believe that the people, horses, objects, and events were not in that moment but were more like recordings or even ripples through time.

Developing Perception through Time

It seems that precognition often arises during peak moments—situations when our psychic senses become heightened due to some form of danger or a huge emotional outpouring. These abilities can and do change our lives, and not always in the obvious ways. For me, seeing and experiencing the future has been an extremely rare occurrence and thus more powerful because of it. I have also only rarely tried to draw upon or use this ability and that too has been a positive choice for me. However, you may consider it worthwhile to develop your precognition, perhaps even to the point where you are able to prove, at least to yourself, that time and space are not as they seem. Therefore I'm going to look at some ways of developing the ability.

I have discussed the main ways that precognition generally arises, such as through dreams, remote viewing, scrying, and out-of-body experiences. All of these methods can be developed and, in fact, each can benefit the other. I believe that remote viewing and scrying are really flip sides of the same coin; they are both methods used to enhance our visual psi abilities. It seems, from history and personal experience, that scrying helps in the forming of visions, while remote viewing uses a structured format that helps gain more accurate and workable results. Combining them might involve staring into a reflective surface while going through a checklist of elements about a given target, which may be a specific future event or the general unfolding of world events in a particular locale. I advise working with a partner if you want to explore this kind of perception; that way, there will be a clearer sense that you have connected with the correct target. There are many different remote-viewing protocols, but most have a very basic structure. You may also find the simple protocol from Chapter 2 useful.

Once you have achieved some degree of success with the out-of-body state, you may wish to explore traveling to past and even future events in a more tangible way. Start with simple, specific targets like a social event or something related to your day-to-day life. Experiencing precognition through an OBE is a different process from working with remote viewing, since the nature of the OBE opens up other possibilities, such as coming across unexpected people, places, and events that can distract you. It also seems to me that, because the out-of-body experience is so much more intense, in the sense that you feel totally separate from your normal understanding of the world, it requires a greater amount of energy and focus to control it. Nearly every time I have experienced something precognitive in nature, I have realised it during the experience, which I believe is due to the energy involved and, in my case, the cerulean-blue cast of my vision.

One of the key factors when wanting to access information outside of linear time is to break down your belief in how time operates. If you find yourself out of the body and you start to think about time in the same way you think about space, you will find that your consciousness reacts and new abilities begin to open up. It is as if you are rewiring your understanding and, by doing so, you open the door to new experiences. It took me a long time to begin to see the idea of perception across time as being possible. It still remains a complex and mysterious area to me, but one that is all the more exciting because of it.

It seems likely that as we learn more about the nature of time, space, and consciousness, the greater the potential becomes that we will be able to use this knowledge for a greater benefit to humanity. Maybe there will be ways to heighten the nature of our precognitive sense to such a degree that we would become aware when we are in mortal danger, or if a major event such as a natural disaster is about to take place. There are already many reports of people having this kind of awareness, yet at present we don't have enough of an understanding of the nature of precognition to really utilise it.

Within the world of fiction, there are many references to seeing the future and the possible impact on our world. "The Minority Report," by Philip K. Dick, treats the idea of precognition in the setting of a future society where murder has been eradicated through the abilities of three "precogs" or precognitive people. Yet the story also raises questions about a society that attempts to create a utopia while controlling its citizens, as well as the issue of free will, which is a key area when we imply that there could be such an ability as precognition. Most of us like to believe that we have choice and that our lives are not simply running along a set track. Leaving aside the psychological question of whether or not there is such a thing as free will, the way I approach this is to look at these future perceptions as *potential* futures. We could even view the precognition as an effect caused by the course of events and the choices we make. If we look at it this way, precognition actually becomes a kind of interaction with your own life. In fact, some remote viewers and scientists believe that precognitive perception may be something like a memory from the future, almost as if your future self is sending the information back to your past self.

Obviously many of these ideas are very hard to fully apprehend, but they offer different ways of looking at precognition that don't negate the notion of free will. They also don't contradict what we know about physics. Of course, those who see time and space as being meaningless on the other planes of reality may have no issue with these concepts. I often hear the idea that in the "spirit world," there is no past, present, or future. Maybe these other levels, if they exist in a literal way, are in fact the ground plan of this reality. Maybe quantum physics will uncover a way that consciousness and reality are part of the same process and dependent in some sense upon each other.

All of these ideas take us to the next level, an area outside of objective scientific understanding. Yet it is in these areas of the subjective that science and new ideas are propelled forward.

13

THE NEXT LEVEL: LIFE AFTER DEATH

The greatest implication of the out-of-body experience is its suggestion that consciousness is not dependent upon the brain and therefore can continue after physical death. This means that the OBE can directly address the oldest and most fundamental questions of human existence, the very essence of spiritual philosophies across the world: Do we have a soul? What lies beyond death? Using the processes in this book, you can attempt your own exploration of the nature of the afterlife, or possibly even connect with loved ones who have passed on, should you wish to.

The out-of-body experience offers us a way to experience a deeper spiritual reality in our lives now, a vision of unconditional love and freedom beyond this world. This level of reality is available not only to those who have stood at the brink of death in the near-death experience, but also to those who have the courage and determination to lift up their consciousness beyond the limitations of their everyday lives and open their eyes to the wonders that lie beyond the body.

Evidence for an Afterlife

The "afterlife" is in many ways an unfortunate term, since it implies that the other levels of reality only exist at the next stage of transformation, after physical death, yet I have seen within my own experiences that this is not the case. In some of my most profound OBEs, I have glimpsed levels of reality populated by beings who I believe may once have lived among us, yet now live on in a state of renewed, pure consciousness.

There is a term often used by scientists, "the convergence of evidence," which basically means multiple kinds of proof, coming from many different angles and disciplines, that all point to the same conclusion. When this convergence exists, it becomes increasingly likely that the idea being looked at is true. It seems to me that what we are dealing with when it comes to the issue of life after physical death is a convergence of evidence. With work in the fields of parapsychology, quantum physics, and near-death research coming to many of the same conclusions, it seems harder and harder to dismiss the possibility that there is some form of continuation of individual consciousness after death.

The near-death experience

Near-death experiences (NDEs), which I have touched upon earlier in this book, offer evidence in a scientific sense as well as a personal sense that there is a deeply spiritual nature to the universe—not a religious nature or even a moral one, but simply a sense that at our core we are all connected via a vast network of consciousness that seems to exist or interpenetrating this reality. This boundless awareness, experienced by millions as pure white light or unconditional love, has been called God, the source of everything.

Whatever we believe it to be, it's clear that many people experience something life-changing and healing in these moments at the edge of death. In virtually any NDE description, we find a deeply held conviction that we are more than our physical bodies and that death is no more than a transition from one state of being to another.

Ghosts and spirits

Parapsychology offers key evidence of life after physical death through research into ghosts and hauntings. In their most basic form, ghosts or apparitions are figures, forms, or images that someone sees, for which there is no physical explanation. However, this in itself proves little. What is needed in these cases is some verifiable evidence.

For example, in the building in which I spent most of my youth, a mother and daughter moved in shortly after the death of an elderly lady. They had no initial awareness of who had lived in their apartment before them, yet almost as soon as they arrived, they began to see an old lady walking through their rooms. She did not pay any attention to the new residents and would simply appear, walk through the kitchen, and vanish. This happened so frequently that the daughter became very frightened. In an effort to find out the history of the apartment, the girl's mother approached my mother, who had known the previous resident. My mother was amazed to hear an accurate description of the old woman, down to fine details of her clothing.

This story is just the experience of a few people in my local community, and can be largely dismissed in the context of science since there is no tangible proof, but stories like this one do offer a starting point for deeper and more scientifically controlled exploration.

When it comes to ghosts and spirits, it's commonly believed that some are conscious or self-aware in some way, and able to interact with observers under the right conditions, while others are not. The latter, often called "residual" hauntings, are more like recordings left by high levels of emotion or by a deceased person's connection to a particular site. The old woman from my childhood apartment block seems to fit well with the idea of an unconscious (residual) recording. She never reacted to those around her or gave any impression that she knew what she was doing.

In my own life, I have seen two apparitions fully visible with my physical eyes—the first when I was very young and the second at sixteen with a close friend. Both took place in the same apartment building mentioned above. In both my experiences, the apparition seemed very aware of its surroundings and seemed to be trying on some level to communicate. I wasn't able to really understand their message, but these experiences did suggest to me that there may be a continuation of consciousness beyond the physical. The first experience took place when I was very young, maybe five or seven years old. I saw a tall humanoid figure standing in the doorway to the flat in which I lived. It remained motionless, yet seemed to convey a sense of something profound simply through its presence. I remember the feeling of terror that this apparition evoked in my young mind—not because it was actually threatening in any way, more that it was such a shock to my sense of reality. The second of these experiences involved an orblike form around the size of a basketball, glowing green. I was with my best friend at the time, yet we weren't fearful; we simply accepted it and felt generally very positive about the experience. It is very hard to describe how we got the impression it was trying to communicate, but in the feelings and impressions that arose, we got a sense our thoughts were being guided. It seemed like a telepathic link rather than anything verbal.

Many people believe that orbs—the blurry circular marks or balls of light—which appear on many digital photographs are in fact spirits. I remain unconvinced by this, since I have enough experience with photography to understand that particles of dust or water can easily make these kinds of impressions. However, my own out-of-body perceptions and the experiences mentioned above leave me wondering if the true nature of spirits might actually be something not dissimilar to the orb concept—in other words, floating spheres of some kind of energy or awareness. Many writers and psychics over the years have also claimed that the true nature of spirits is something akin to an orb. In many of my own OBEs, I have also taken an orblike form, which felt very much like a natural state, more natural even than the humanoid form that is also common in my experiences.

Whether or not you believe that ghosts exist, there is strong evidence generally accepted by both skeptics and proponents that there is a relationship between ghost sightings and electromagnetic fields (EMFs). Skeptics claim that these fields may stimulate the temporal lobes of the brain, resulting in hallucinations. Proponents either claim that strong EMFs are often found in the presence of ghostly activity, or alternately that the field does stimulate the brain but this actually aids in the process of perceiving the spirit. Again, it seems to come down to whether or not what people see can be shown to have some objective basis in fact. Some cases support this, while others don't. However, the quality of an individual case is of more importance than the fact that some aspects can be put down to weaknesses in human perception. If the majority of the evidence put forward is factual and difficult to obtain, this still remains hugely supportive of the argument that there is something objective taking place.

In some cases, trained observers claim to have witnessed tangible physical phenomena, such as objects moving and energies and forms moving around in front of multiple witnesses. All of these different factors lend some credibility to the idea that spirits exist, but more research is needed, in a controlled and genuinely scientific way, if we are to gain solid evidence that would convince a skeptic.

Past-life memories

The theory of reincarnation also suggests that a continuation of consciousness may take place. Descriptions of past lives, especially those that arise from young children, provide intriguing clues. In many of these cases, the child has been able to accurately describe large amounts of detail from the previous life, including the circumstances of their death.

One recent example is Cameron Macauley, a boy from Glasgow, Scotland. Beginning at about the age of two, he claimed that he had lived before, on the remote island of Barra in the Outer Hebrides off the northwest coast of Scotland. He described a white house where he lived with his mother, father, brothers, and sisters. This house had a view of the beach where the plane from the mainland would land. He also described the surrounding area, such as rock pools and a gate to the beach. He was able to give the name "Robertson" as the surname of his father, although he may have been inaccurate about the first name. The case is a strong one, since the boy is quite young, but describes living in a remote place that it is highly unlikely he would have any conscious knowledge of. He is also able to offer details of his life on the island that are very difficult to explain.

In adults, too, there are those who have been able to give the details of a previous life. Cameron is far from unique in his perceptions. In fact, I don't include this case as an exceptional example, but more of an everyday one. It illustrates how "normal" people with no paranormal interest or background are confronted with situations that make it hard to reject the notion of consciousness surviving death. Similar cases exist worldwide, and are especially common when the person from the previous life is thought to have died violently or accidentally.

Does this mean that we have a spirit that simply moves from one body to the next? Or is it possible to receive information from a remote source, such as the mind of someone who has passed, much the same as with telepathy with the living? While I don't see the idea of a literal soul or spirit as having much weight when viewed through the lens of what we have learnt about psychic abilities, I do see that the forms of experience that our senses and awareness create offer something very close to a spirit. It becomes simply a matter of how we interpret what we experience. If the brain is in some ways like a receiver, as discussed earlier, then reincarnation would simply be the receiving of information from the mind of someone no longer physically alive. Maybe this information is stored in the interconnected nature of the universe, in some kind of morphic field, or in the akashic records. At this point in time, we simply don't know. But as physics and other areas of science learn more, we are given clues to how our own experiences might relate to our unfolding knowledge of the universe.

Accessing the Transphysical Levels

You will find a technique for reaching the transphysical levels or planes in the appendix (see page 208), but next let's explore some of the important factors beyond techniques and consider the awe-inspiring possibilities these levels hold.

Accessing levels beyond physical existence, in my experience, is best achieved through preparation over an extended period of weeks, during which a focus on someone who has passed over can be developed. It is best to have a particular goal in mind, such as connecting with a loved one, or, more generally, with those in the in-between states who may not be fully conscious of their circumstances. Based on research into reincarnation and my own experiences, the period up to sixteen months after death is the most effective time to do this work, especially if the deceased experienced a violent or unexpected death. If you are already exploring being out of your body, you may find that you are naturally drawn to a person who has passed on.

Your energy levels, focus, and goal should be paramount. What you are attempting to do will have a profound impact on your life, should you succeed, and is one of the factors that extinguishes the fear of physical death. When I first encountered someone who had recently died while out of my body, I was filled with a sense of awe, disbelief, and relief all at the same time. It was not until that moment that I really believed that consciousness continues—and not just to an afterlife, but maybe to a new physical life as well. I reached that point after hearing a lecture on the subject and considered for the first time that we can use the OBE as a tangible way to investigate for ourselves whether there is some continuation of consciousness.

I believe it is quite possible to access these nonphysical realities; it simply requires a degree of focus and energy that the more general out-of-body states do not. It is a matter of stretching your awareness and energies further than you ever have before. I would break down the process as follows:

- Step 1: Begin with meditation during the morning and in the evening. Prepare with a visualisation practice and thirty to forty minutes in the Ganzfeld state.

- Step 2: If you are able, induce the vibrational state but do not exit your body right away. Build up the state, allowing the energy to reach a kind of critical mass, and then allow yourself to lift up.

- Step 3: Keep lifting, trying not to focus on your environment. Focus on your goal of reaching a particular person and try to keep the momentum going until you sense that you have reached as far as you need to, or can.

- Step 4: At this point, you may experience a connection with the person in a whole range of ways—from images connected to them to what appears to be their physical appearance. This is a very subjective point in the process, and you should try to allow whatever form it takes to happen as naturally as possible. Don't force the process or cloud things with preconceptions about what will happen.

- Step 5: You may find that the process will come to a conclusion in its own time and you will regain body awareness again. If not, you can focus on your body and request in your mind to return. This should be all that is needed to return, as with other OBEs.

While I have personally found this approach effective, you may want to adapt it a little if you have experience in other areas such as mediumship. Those who have this kind of background tend to find that linking with these levels is much easier than it is for the average person. If you have had other paranormal experiences, you might also find that your sense of awareness is more attuned. Whatever the case, use my program as the blueprint, but don't be scared to change elements and combine other techniques from the appendix if you've found they tend to be more effective for you.

My experiences with the transphysical levels

The energy that arose in my body was different from normal; it felt distant, even foreign, as well as subtle and hard to define. I seemed to sink into the experience, like my body was melting away and all that was left was a strange grayish mist, beyond which I could make out maybe a hundred or more figures moving along what seemed like a boundary. There was nothing visible holding them back, but they were all spread out along a sharply defined line. Behind them was a source of light, silhouetting them in relation to my vantage point. There was also a yellowish radiant light coming from the figures themselves. It was hard to make out clothing or genders. They appeared to be human and to know where they were going, but they seemed to have no awareness of me. I sensed that some of them might have been there for some time.

Was this an "in-between" location, between our physical world and an adjacent one? I don't know, but somehow it didn't seem like the fully "aware" levels of radiant light that we might imagine when thinking of an afterlife. As with other experiences on this level, I was unable to make these figures aware of me, or get close enough to communicate. The experience concluded with me being drawn back to my body after I sensed I had seen enough.

More recently, another experience took place when I saw a truck crash and saw the consciousness of the person in the truck seem to exit his body. In the following days, I searched online for news of the crash in the general area of North America where I had guessed it might have happened, and I did find a report that matched what I had witnessed in my out-of-body state.

I couldn't come to any definite conclusions from these experiences. Each one was a fleeting glimpse of what may have been the levels beyond our physical understanding, but the exact nature of those levels, and the beings I encountered there, is still a mystery.

During the writing of this chapter, I had an additional experience of the transphysical levels, in which I felt myself lifting up from my body through layers and layers of what appeared to be delicate misty moments of reality— like spiritual strata falling away as I passed through. With each new layer, rich colour flowed around me, like the pure colours hidden within sunlight revealed through the prism of my consciousness, before I finally reached a place of rich oranges and reds. It seemed like a kind of "summerland," a place in which our human awareness is made primal again, as if the raw environments of the Earth are here separated into their parts or elements, much like the colours in sunlight. Again I was aware of people at a distance. I felt different; I had a very strong sense of a body here. I felt like a spirit being, not the point of consciousness that sometimes dominates my perception.

It's easy to imagine that if the peoples of the past experienced something like this, why they would have put forward such elaborate metaphysical explanations for the origins of the universe and spiritual immortality. I remember my first teacher, when I was still in my teens, telling me his view that the rich, vibrant colours of Indian costume or the beauty of the grand stained glass of the world's cathedrals mirror the radiance of the layered reality beyond this one. These textiles and works of art are attempts to come closer to the divine or infinite. My own experiences have allowed me to witness the universe with my entire consciousness, not via the filters of my senses, but through a direct apprehension.

The Summerlands

The concept of the afterlife having an appearance much like an idyllic Earth environment, enveloped in light and vivid colour, has entered the popular imagination and is now common in movies as well as literature. The term *summerlands* has come to public awareness via the various Neopagan and Earth-centered spiritual philosophies, but like much of New Age and contemporary spiritual thinking, it has its roots in much older belief systems including some Native American beliefs.

Emanuel Swedenborg, a Swedish scientist who later in life became a mystic, described summerland-type environments as part of his otherworldly journeys. Swedenborg has fascinated me for many years; I would often walk past the Swedenborg Society or the Swedish Church minutes from where I grew up in London and think of him. He spent most of his life in London and actually died there; he was buried in the Swedish Church at its original location before his body was moved to Uppsala in Sweden.

But beyond Swedenborg's impact on descriptions of the transphysical levels, he was also well known for his psychic abilities. There is a famous story that tells of a startling experience of his, which in modern terms sounds very much like remote viewing. In 1759, Swedenborg had just arrived in Göteborg, Sweden, after a trip to England. Shortly after, he was having dinner with a group of friends and peers when he suddenly "became aware" of a fire raging in Stockholm close by his home there. He was visibly concerned by this, since all of his most valuable manuscripts and possessions were there. The story goes that he exclaimed, "Thank God! The fire is extinguished the third door from my house."[1] At the time, long before the instant communications we have today, there is no feasible way he could have known of a fire in Stockholm, some 250 miles away, at the time it was happening. When reports of the fire did reach Göteborg, it became clear that Swedenborg's statements had been accurate, and his reputation continued to grow.

C. W. Leadbeater is another individual who has had a major influence on the popular conception of the afterlife and the astral planes. An influential Theosophist and noted psychic artist, he described a plane of reality he called the summerland, but in his case referenced from Spiritualist ideas. He saw it as an illusory level of the astral plane, where the dead could spend "a number of years."[2]

In fact, the summerland concept appears in many traditions as a kind of in-between level that the dead occupy as they go through a transformation to the higher, less physical levels. It is not surprising to me because, if consciousness does continue, as it seems to, then what environment would be more natural for our awareness to surround itself with than the beauty and grandeur of an Earthlike landscape? If this level is the first step in our spiritual evolution after death, it seems a very fitting one.

My own experience of the summerland levels happened quite early on in my OBEs. I lifted out of my body to see the subtle light of the moon coming through my window. There was nothing to suggest about my physical surroundings. I then began to feel myself rising up at a very fast rate. I don't know what caused this; it seemed to come from nowhere, leaving me startled and surprised. A moment later, I was met with a vision of indescribable beauty. I lifted up over a vast meadow of vivid green, infused with rich amber undertones. Surrounding the meadow were trees, rich with colour and foliage, reds and deep greens. Above was an intense indigo-blue sky, highlighted by billowing white clouds.

It took a few moments to become accustomed to the scene, since my perceptions were not used to such grand visions of nature. Yet it seemed so peaceful and somehow familiar. I wanted to find somewhere to rest and take in the beauty and feel the warm energy that pervaded every leaf, flower, and blade of grass. Almost as soon as I thought it, I felt myself lift up again and float forward, through a shallow avenue between some trees, finally drifting to the ground at the foot of a large tree at the center of a clearing. As I sat there, the warmth of the energy seemed to rise and swirl around my body. I felt any tension or resistance evaporate like mist. My sense of well-being grew and I could feel in that moment a smile arising from a deep inner peace. There was nothing but the sensation of awe, beauty, and peace.

I don't know how long I spent there, but it felt long enough to let go of much of the anguish that existed in some part of my being. It was a place of pure catharsis and release, but it was time to return, so I let myself drift up into the air. I wondered how I would relate to the city and the world again. Moments later, I was back in my body, yet I didn't open my eyes. I tried to hold the image of this wonderful summerland in my mind. I didn't know if I'd ever return there, and I wanted to hold some sense of the awe of that place in my consciousness, to take it with me into the world.

The Out-of-Body Experience and Spiritual Development

Throughout the ages, mankind has sought to understand the nature of the spiritual realm, to know whether we truly are immortal and, if so, what awaits us on the other side, the next level of existence. The out-of-body experience, like no other practice, can give us personal, tangible, and life-changing answers to our spiritual questions. It can lead us down a path toward a fulfillment of our spiritual longing. So profound is this experience that, after more than two decades of exploration, I still pause by a roadside or in a silent circle of trees and sense the life running through my being, alive and unfettered by any of the limitations of physical reality, totally and completely free. And even more than that, I have a sense that not only is this state of being eternal, it is also outside of time altogether. I have little doubt that if we wish to learn who we really are, to reach the core of ourselves, the OBE is one of the most powerful ways that we can do it.

Over the years, I have practiced many spiritual disciplines. I have found that as I've matured spiritually, I've slowly stripped away the unnecessary beliefs that come along with many spiritual practices. I have learnt that with any insight into the transphysical, there is a responsibility not to be drawn into the trap of certainty or exaggerated beliefs. The OBE has reminded me of this, for despite the many ideas that are repeated in New Age circles, direct experience cuts through them with a clear crystalline precision. As I outlined in my first book, *Avenues of the Human Spirit*, my understanding of spirituality is of an inner core, an awareness, free from negative influences, coercion, and conflict. It is the part of each individual that is most free, the part that is closest to ourselves if we were truly our own architects.

If we focus our attention on this simple, unfettered core and work with nothing that does not enhance our understanding of this simplicity, we can progress much more truthfully toward our personal spiritual maturity. We must fill our lives with nurturing influences, the approaches that are simplest and which encourage us to look deeply at the parts of ourselves that are always there—our heartbeat, our breath, the stillness behind our emotions and thoughts. These are the places to put our attention; from these will arise a genuine spiritual understanding. It is good to remember that the Buddha was not a Buddhist; he was an explorer into spiritual nature. This is what we must become.

The out-of-body experience was a purifying process for me. It took a boy from the inner city, defined and limited by his environment, and slowly dissolved those limits. Each time I left my body, I was brought into contact with a pure perception, far from the preconceptions of my culture and up-bringing. Suddenly the importance of the superficial choices that had domi-nated my life until that point became of no importance. I gained a powerful sense of will and drive because I could see that the things that dominated the lives of many of those around me led nowhere. In fact, they often led to self-destructive patterns.

Reading, learning, and experiencing through the OBE essentially re-educated me to see great benefit in growth-based ideas, rather than ones that lead to bad health and a limited worldview. Much of Western culture is based upon destructive patterns like drinking heavily and overconsuming in terms of food as well as resources and products. These are the things we are socialized to crave, yet they bring us little lasting benefit. The OBE, on the other hand, has brought about a sense of peace, happiness, and freedom in my life. I am not just talking about a sense of wanting to improve; I mean a total shift in the things I am drawn to and what I want in my life. Being aware of the actions we take on a day-to-day level is often missed when we undertake a new practice—the result being that we reach a point where we are in a state of conflict between the new, beneficial ideas that have come into our lives and the desire to fill our lives superficially through things.

Some traditions discourage the active practice of out-of-body explora-tion, believing that these things should arise naturally through more general spiritual practices. In this context, the OBE would be considered a *siddhi* or psychic/magical power that arises in the spiritually advanced. While I understand the reasoning for focusing on the meditational practices first, it seems to me that in Western cultures, exploring the OBE relates well to our understanding of the world and our cultural heritage. Both clearly lead to a flowering of awareness, as I have shown, so there seems little doubt that both paths are valid and workable.

Whether you are interested in spiritual development, developing practical psychic awareness, reaching a loved one who has passed on, or some goal totally your own, I hope that this book will not just allow you to achieve out-of-body experiences, but also, through this profound nonphysical state, to find a sense of spiritual evolution, inner peace, and freedom. As we stand at the edge of a world of infinite possibility, it is almost impossible not to be humbled and filled with a sense of how small we really are, yet how much potential exists within us. Many of the limits that we place on ourselves are arbitrary, and it is only by experiencing what lies beyond them that we are able to understand this. As you step out into the unknown in the tradition of the great seekers throughout the ages, fear only that which diminishes the human spirit. Remember that I am just like you; I am standing next to you in the street, sitting beside you on the bus. We are all human beings, searching and learning. The beauty of this shared humanity is that we can understand each other and attain the same heights. Look into the mirror and see greatness; see the expanse that is your consciousness. You are free and limitless, a child of the universe, looking with wonder at the source.

Epilogue

This book is the result of nearly a quarter of a century of out-of-body exploration. Within that time I have undergone many changes, both to my opinion of who I am and my view of the nature of reality itself. The writing of this, my second book, has been surprising on so many levels. Surprising because I signed my publishing contract with Llewellyn within a matter of weeks of signing the contract on my first book, *Avenues of the Human Spirit*. Somehow they were meant to be together—the first a philosophical and autobiographical journey into spirituality and the nature of the transformation the OBE can initiate, the second, the one you have just read, a detailed and scientifically inspired guide to allow you to undertake a similar journey for yourself.

When I look back to the boy of thirteen or fourteen reading about the wonders of out-of-body experiences for the first time, I imagine this book having a similar impact as the books I read as a young teenager. I can see myself dreaming and full of motivation and excitement at the possibility of doing something miraculous. And even when I sat down to begin writing, I felt that sense of excitement return; it is clear that this book is so much more than my young mind imagined.

I always knew I would write this book, because I always knew that I was charting territory that few others had explored. I knew that part of my role in life was to offer others something of these awe-inspiring experiences, a way to access a part of themselves that they never may have imagined before. And while that sense of awe and wonder might be driven by little more than curiosity for many, I know that over time these experiences can open up the whole personality to a profound and deeply important change.

Writing a book is not simply about communicating a set of ideas; it is about raising awareness, lifting someone from the everyday and mundane to a point at which they are inspired and reminded of the vast possibilities awaiting them in the mysteries and wonders of the world. We need not seek fulfillment in the superficial aspects of life. We can grow through our own unique experiences; we can live in the world fully and without compromise. In my understanding, anything I write should be about that sense of growth and change.

While working with the techniques and ideas in this book, I hope that you will record everything that happens each day in your journal—even if it feels like nothing happened—as I have done. Explore through your journal the impact and power of your journey. If you have a powerful experience, note how you got there, so that you will be able to reach it again. And please do share your experiences with me via my website, www.grahamnicholls.com.

Use this book as a launching pad to explore the full potential of consciousness. We are still taking our first steps in our understanding of the vast range of possibilities that exists. I have written this book with the spirit of inquiry, rather than dogma and belief. I hope that you will take something from that, and realise that it was only by letting go of my preconceptions and looking with open eyes that I was able to fully experience not just the out-of-body state, but life itself. I wish you transformative and life-enhancing experiences.

Appendix

TECHNIQUES AND APPROACHES

How to Use This Section

In the following pages, you will find detailed techniques divided into their respective categories. The reason for this is so that you can easily select the most relevant techniques for your personality and skills (based on the questionnaire in Chapter 4). There are three main stages, a relaxation technique, a vibrational state technique, and a main technique for your type (visual, auditory, intellectual, or physical) The relaxation techniques are generally suitable for everyone, but I have highlighted who will likely gain most from each one. Next you will find Vibrational State Techniques, as the vibrational state is common in around half of all people who have out-of-body experiences. Please pay special attention to the G-Technique, as in my coaching and workshops I have found it highly effective, especially for physically fit people used to practices such as Hatha Yoga. The top level techniques in each section are for Waking people, while Type 2, or Sleeping/Dream people's techniques are marked Type 2. If you fall somewhere between these two categories, you should select the method that most fits your type, plus the sensory category (visual, auditory, intellectual, or physical). You might find it helpful to make a list as you go of the techniques you select to use.

Relaxation Techniques

Virtually all techniques for leaving the body, from both traditional eso-teric literature and more modern approaches, begin with a period of relax-ation. Body stage relaxation and biofeedback relaxation are two of the best forms. Body stage relaxation is a widely used and well-known technique that involves slowly tensing then relaxing each part of your body in turn until all muscle tension is gone. You might begin with your toes and slowly move to each muscle group, letting go and breathing deeply, until you can no longer feel any resistance. Biofeedback relaxation, as discussed earlier, uses a piece of electronic equipment called a biofeedback device and is a very powerful tool for someone new to relaxation and meditation. The device measures physiological data such as heart rate or skin temperature as indica-tors of tension and transmits an audible tone. The user learns to bring down the tone, and thus the indicators of tension, through controlled breathing and other relaxation techniques. You can literally hear the results of your relaxation process. This "feedback" helps you learn to relax and, after practice, you will be able to achieve the same results without the device.

Deep Breathing Technique

Good for: Everyone, but especially those new to relaxation techniques
Consistent full breathing has a tangible effect on the body, resulting in a deep level of relaxation. It is the single most powerful way to relax and

relieve stress; therefore many of the processes I describe include some degree of breath work. To begin to understand the relationship between your level of relaxation and your breathing, here is a simple technique.

- Step 1: Find a comfortable place and sit down. I recommend a posture that you know you can sit in for an extended period without loss of circulation or discomfort. While many people attempt to go straight into the lotus posture or other yogic asanas (postures), this can be counterproductive when learning, because if the posture becomes painful, you will not be able to continue or benefit from what you are doing.

- Step 2: Now focus on your normal breathing rhythm. Don't try to adjust or slow your breath at this point; just become aware of the natural speed and depth at which you normally breathe. Continue until you feel totally at ease and comfortable with this level of calm stillness.

- Step 3: Now take a deeper breath and exhale naturally and comfortably. Continue breathing in deeply and exhaling deeply until it becomes second nature.

- Step 4: Continue as in step 3, but now hold the breath for a few seconds longer. Use this moment of stillness on the in-breath to imagine your state of awareness growing and your tensions vanishing. Let the breath out slowly. Continue like this, but begin to gradually slow your breathing.

- Step 5: Find a natural, deep, slow in-and-out tempo. You may want to count the seconds so that it is easier to gauge how long the complete cycle takes. By counting in this way, you may also find that you can slow the breathing cycle even more, with practice. If you find counting a distraction, simply trust your intuition with regard to the length of the cycle and slowly build from there. The goal is simply to reach a state of deep, slow breathing, which will result in a deeper level of relaxation and calm.

Presence (Mindfulness) Technique

Good for: Everyone, but especially those new to relaxation techniques

The term *presence* has become popular in recent years with the success of books like *The Power of Now* by Eckhart Tolle, but the idea is in fact a very old one. It is especially found in Eastern religions such as Hinduism and Buddhism and is essentially a form of mindfulness. Mindfulness is a state of full awareness while being detached from the tides and flows of your emotional and mental self. In this powerful state of mind, the very idea of relaxation becomes less important, since you are less prone to emotional ups and downs and thus require fewer processes to deal with stress.

Finding presence or mindfulness is especially useful for people who are confronted with stressful situations in their day-to-day lives. On the most basic level, it allows you to gain detachment from the stress of commuting to work, for example, or dealing with a difficult coworker. For this reason, cultivating a sense of detached awareness will only benefit the process of relaxing and stilling the mind.

I have found that cultivating mindfulness in relation to the out-of-body experience makes leaving the body much easier. However, it is important to also cultivate the psychic and creative aspects of your nature. Awareness that is too inwardly focused can make perceiving on the psychic level harder. As with most things, there is a balance to be struck. The inward stillness of meditation, presence, and mindfulness is key to leading an aware life, but we must also remember to engage fully, with vitality and creativity.

- Step 1: The next time you are on a busy train or in a situation that you find stressful, take time to observe what is going on around you. Don't get emotionally engaged with the situation; try to detach and see it for what it is. Look at the people around you and explore what their attitudes and reactions may be stemming from. If there is a person who bothers you, ask yourself what need he or she is expressing underneath that you perceive as anger, frustration, or negative attitude.

- Step 2: Empathise with this person, or try to think of the stressful situation as simply the result of a set of occurrences. For example, a train is stressful because of the physical impact it has on you—the heat, the noise, the cramped conditions, and so on. Accept that these conditions are simply factors that impact your body and lead to a (largely automatic) reaction. You do not have a choice in the situation, but you do have a choice in how you feel.

- Step 3: Accept the situation and look for its positive sides. For instance, the train is cheap and convenient, and you will soon reach your destination. Realise that what you are experiencing is temporary and may have few actual negative elements. You may realise that you are letting the situation affect you too much, and are having a more intense emotional reaction than is logical or helpful.

- Step 4: Change the way you are reacting to the situation. Draw upon your change in perspective and reflect this in your physiology. Slow your breathing, slow your movements, tone down your emotional reactions, and explore the possibilities available to you. Sometimes the right choice may be to immediately exit the stressful situation, but more often we simply need to regain some perspective—which is what mindfulness is all about.

Relaxation Massage Technique

Good for: Everyone, but especially Physical people

Even if you are not working with a partner, having a professional massage before an OBE session may help you to reach a deeper level of physical relaxation. Many gyms and health spas offer massages, so you may be able to include them in a general health program. Some gyms also have saunas on-site, which are another way of helping the body feel revitalized and relaxed, and can help overcome the stress that colder climates can put on the body.

Below are instructions for you giving a massage to a partner; the partner can then repeat this process with you, or use this technique on himself or herself.

- Step 1: Work with a partner with whom you're comfortable physically. Your partner should lie down on his or her stomach and breathe slowly and evenly, trying to clear the mind of any distracting thoughts.

- Step 2: You will begin by focusing on your partner's back, shoulders, and base of the neck. These areas usually hold the most tension and prevent full relaxation. Start by slowly rotating your thumbs at the points on either side of the base of the head. You will feel the point of the skull on either side of the neck; apply pressure just under those points. You may want to place your hands on the sides of your partner's head to position your thumbs better.

- Step 3: Now move down the neck to the top of the shoulders and firmly but gently massage the muscles that run across the top of the shoulders.

- Step 4: Now move down to the shoulder blades; for many people, this is where the bulk of their knots and tension are located. You may find it useful to bring your partner's arm across their back a little, which will open up the shoulder blade and allow you to work out all the tension located there.

- Step 5: Move down the spine, working the muscles on either side as you go, until you reach the base of the spine. Here you will feel the two points that the pelvis often makes, which look like dimples in the back. With your thumbs, push and rotate the area around these points.

- Step 6: Now repeat what you have done so far, but in reverse. When you reach the shoulders, move down the right arm, paying attention to the muscles as you go. When you reach the hand, apply pressure to the center of the palm with your thumb for a few seconds. Then move to the small, round muscle just above and next to the thumb and below the index finger. Again, apply pressure and rotate it for a minute or so.

- Step 7: Repeat the above process on the other arm and hand.

- Step 8: Return to the base of the spine and move straight up. Apply more energy to the shoulder blades before ending at the base of the skull.

Conscious Sleep Technique (Yoga Nidra)

Good for: Type 2 (sleeping/dream) people

For those who identified themselves as a Type 2 (sleeping/dream) person in Chapter 4, I advise working with a relaxation method that utilises the hypnagogic or "in-between" state, which is the point just before sleep when images and impressions from your day arise. Generally, these people have less need for a relaxation method, since by working when you're about to fall asleep, you are already in a state of relaxation. However, you can still benefit from this technique, since it results in deeper sleep and also reduced stress, which ultimately benefits your OBE training. It is based on the traditional Yoga Nidra practice, but with slight variations for our purposes. It involves consciously feeling the process of falling asleep, but as you go through each stage, you maintain a distant awareness.

- Step 1: Get into bed or into a position where you are comfortable and could easily fall asleep. Close your eyes. Allow the images and concerns of the day to arise. Let them drift into your mind and then let them go. Let all the emotions arise and then subside. Try to remain detached from what you see and feel.

- Step 2: Now allow the abstract images, colours, and shapes that appear on the eyelids to come to the fore. This is called the hypnagogic state, but in this context you remain still and conscious, observing from a distance as if you are centered at your core.

- Step 3: Now allow yourself to enter into a state of deeper relaxation, but again, remain aware and engaged. Your body and your everyday mind are essentially asleep, yet your core self is aware, conscious, and centered.

- Step 4: With practice, you will reach a state of "mind awake/ body asleep". Leaving the body from this state is far easier. Focus your attention into the expanse of awareness.

- Step 5: Let your self or centre of awareness phase or move to another place distant from your body. Simply focusing in this way, and using a simple cue such as "up" or "leave my body" will often result in an OBE.

Vibrational State Techniques

Achieving the vibrational state is one of the key abilities in the development of fully conscious out-of-body experiences, whether you are a Type 1 (waking/conscious) or a Type 2 (sleeping/dream) person. The following techniques will help you learn to sense and manipulate energy related to the vibrational state and should be used in conjunction with a relaxation technique beforehand and a sensory (visual, auditory, intellectual, or physical) method. If you are a Type 2 Sleeping/Dream person you can still use vibrational state techniques before sleeping, as it does not involve being fully asleep.

Introductory Vibrational State Technique

Good for: Those new to visualisation or energy manipulation techniques

This method should be practiced daily until you can induce the vibrational state effectively. When your visualisation skills have improved, progress on to the more complex techniques.

- Step 1: Hold your hands out in front of you as if you are holding a basketball or beachball. Imagine that in your hands is a glowing ball of light and energy. Try to feel the sensation of pressure between your fingers.

- Step 2: In your imagination, throw the energy ball up into the air. Imagine it stopping and floating at a point above your head.

- Step 3: Close your eyes and, in your mind's eye, see the ball of energy floating there like a small sun. If you are able, feel its heat as well. Continue for a minute or two.

- Step 4: Now imagine that ball of energy becoming compressed, like a source of vast power being forced down into a smaller form and, by doing so, becoming brighter and more powerful.

- Step 5: Now see that compressed, powerful ball buzzing and sparking as if it is going to explode. Can you feel its energy? Move it directly above your head.

- Step 6: Now allow your compressed ball of energy to burst down and become a powerful stream of light and energy surging into your body.

- Step 7: Feel your whole body buzz and vibrate as the energy activates you.

Three-Dimensional Doorway Technique
Good for: Everyone, but especially Visual or Physical people
This is the advanced version of my pyramid meditation (see page 129), focused on inducing a state of heightened energy.

- Step 1: Find the center of your physical room or space. Kneel down there and put your hands out in front of you, touching at the fingertips, palms together, arms fully extended.

- Step 2: Focus on your hands out in front of you and try to project your energy to the point just between your hands. Do this until you begin to see and sense energy generating. (Rubbing your hands briskly together may help you begin to sense the energy.) Spend several half-hour to one-hour sessions working on this until you become intensely aware of your own subtle energies.

· Step 3: Slowly stand, maintaining the energy in front of you. Begin to slowly move your hands apart, drawing the energy with them, until your arms naturally lock. Now focus on the energy flowing in a line in front of you, between your hands. Focus on it and intensify it.

· Step 4: Draw your hands together to meet at the fingertips as before, but this time above your head, forming a triangle with the energy.

· Step 5: Now close your eyes and vividly see the energy in front of you as it flows around the triangle. See it expand until it is in proportion to your body, like a doorway.

· Step 6: Focus on the center of the triangle, then focus on seeing beyond it. In a few moments, you will begin to see or sense some kind of location beyond the boundary of the portal.

· Step 7: Repeat the process until there are three triangular portals around you. Now sense each portal opening, and how this causes their energy to interact.

· Step 8: Now focus your attention on the fourth triangle below your feet, formed by the edges of the others. Once this fourth triangle opens, energy channels will surround you; they will create a fifth portal from their interaction.

· Step 9: The fifth portal will give you access to a high degree of energy that can then be drawn into the body, starting just behind the top of the head and flowing down to the feet. Take a few moments to feel it doing so. The vibrational state often begins with a sensation of pulsing energy flowing into the body as you do this.

- Step 10: To finish, slowly reverse the process and ground yourself into normal reality again.

Sphere Doorway Technique

Good for: Everyone, but especially Intellectual or Visual people

This is probably the hardest of the techniques you will attempt. I advise working with the Three-Dimensional Doorway Technique, above, for a while before you attempt this version. It requires a high level of mental acrobatics.

- Step 1: Imagine a sphere in front of you. I recommend you see it as blue, since this colour has been highly effective for me. See it as around the size of a basketball with a smooth, uniform surface.

- Step 2: Focus on the surface of the sphere, in your mind's eye. Allow it to rotate and move on its axis. Really pay attention to its form as you imagine it floating in space.

- Step 3: Move the mental image around you. Try to move it behind you and still maintain a sense of its presence. Move it above your head, again maintaining a sense of its location and how it feels in that location.

- Step 4: Now bring the sphere back in front of you and see whether it has changed in any way. Focus again on the surface and see the surface begin to become misty or slightly transparent.

- Step 5: This is the part where you will need to hold the visualisation in mind. See the whole surface becoming a doorway, opening up and allowing the energy of the sphere to come through. Your mind will no doubt become a little knotted by the impossibility of a spherical form opening in this way, but stick with it, and don't allow your mind to analyse what is happening.

- Step 6: Allow the energy to flow out of the doorway to surround you or, if you feel heightened enough, into your body. Note the way the energy feels. How does it differ from that of the pyramid? Does it trigger the vibrational state in your body?

- Step 7: To finish, slowly reverse the process and ground yourself into normal reality again.

After a few attempts at this technique, try visualizing two spheres. Go through exactly the same process but let the spheres open, first one then the other. Do the energies mix or affect each other? You can also move the spheres so that they overlap and become totally aligned. This can be very interesting as you, in effect, have two doorways on top of each other.

Sleep Interruption Technique

Good for: Type 2 (sleeping/dream) people

- Step 1: Set an alarm for around two hours before your usual waking time, ideally an alarm that does not jolt you abruptly out of sleep.

- Step 2: Once awake, do not get out of bed. Lie there for a few moments and think back over the dream you were having when awakened, or any other you can remember clearly. Try to sense how you felt physically in the dream. Did you have any body awareness? If so, how did it feel?

- Step 3: Now try shifting your awareness back and forth between the sleep state and the waking state. The Conscious Sleep Technique on page 185 may help with this.

- Step 4: Now try to shift back and forth while gradually doing so faster and going deeper.

- Step 5: As you find yourself in the in-between state, try to hold your awareness in that state. Reach out with your consciousness until you sense energy and vibrations moving around or down into your body and triggering your vibrational state. It may take a few attempts to reach this point.

Home Immersive Approaches

These approaches can be used alongside the other techniques listed here to reach deeper levels of trance. The idea is to build a kind of "toolbox" of methods and systems that not only bring you into trance while you are using them, but also leave a lasting imprint on your unconscious, leading to a higher chance of having an out-of-body experience at a later date. The more you focus your attention on the idea of leaving the body, and the more you become comfortable with this idea, the higher your chances of success.

Ganzfeld Approach

Good for: Type 1 (waking/conscious) and Visual people

This is the process for making a Ganzfeld set-up yourself. I will outline here how to work with Ganzfeld to benefit the OBE. I recommend a thirty- to thirty-five-minute session, following the steps below.

- Step 1: Get comfortable in your chair or recliner, cover your eyes, and turn on the red light and the pink noise. Gaze into the red glow while allowing the sounds to envelope you. Allow your eyes to search in the void in front of you until they become still and you enter a state of inner focus.

- Step 2: Let your everyday thoughts evaporate, and focus on the images and forms that begin to appear in front of you. Let them unfold, and allow yourself to be taken with the images.

- Step 3: You may find that you are perceiving whole scenes and landscapes. Try to place your consciousness fully into the scene.

- Step 4: You may realise that you are out of your body at some point in this process. You may also find that you experience perceptions very much like remote viewing.

Aerial Footage Approach

Good for: Type 1 (waking/conscious), Visual, and Physical people

This approach involves using a large television screen or, even better, a projector. You will need to get hold of some aerial footage, but any footage that gives the impression of flying and weightlessness can be used (see the Resources section of my website, www.grahamnicholls.com). I advise doing a variation of this as a form of meditation each day for around thirty minutes.

- Step 1: Start the footage and stand in front of the screen in a darkened room. Focus on the movement and try to imagine that you are in the scene, floating across clouds and over vast landscapes.

- Step 2: Begin to feel the sensations of the air rushing past and the feeling of your body floating above the ground.

- Step 3: Allow your body to move with the movement on screen. This will probably happen naturally, so do not fight it. Experience the full range of sensations.

- Step 4: Begin to repeat out loud an affirmation such as, "I am able to leave my body and experience this and any landscape I desire."

- Step 5: Now lie back on a bed or in a recliner and close your eyes. Let the images and impressions you have been watching continue to arise in your mind.

- Step 6: Try to shift your awareness so that it syncs with the images you've seen. Focus on the sensations of floating and moving. Allow these sensations to lead naturally into an out-of-body experience.

Techniques for Intellectual People

Mirror Technique

This approach is based upon a form of affirmation.

- Step 1: Before you get into bed to sleep, hold a large mirror in front of you.

- Step 2: Look into your eyes and greet the image in the mirror as your subconscious self. Imagine the image in the mirror as the part of you that can make anything happen.

- Step 3: Ask your subconscious self to cause you to leave your body during the night and to ensure that you have full recall of what you see and do.

- Step 4: Now place the mirror in another room. Lie down, and keep the image of your subconscious self in the mirror in the forefront of your mind as you drift into sleep.

- Step 5: Focus on the location of the mirror and again ask your subconscious self to cause you to leave your body as you sleep and to ensure that you have full recall.

Sunlight Technique

- Step 1: Use the Deep Breathing Technique (see page 180) until you feel totally clear and calm. Now imagine that you are walking to the window of the room and that outside it is a beautiful spring day full of sunshine.

- Step 2: Now imagine yourself opening the windows of the room. Feel the breeze lightly touching your face and feel the warmth of the sun on your skin.

- Step 3: The room that you are in is becoming infused with positivity, light, and peace. Even the everyday objects that you are so familiar with have become somehow lighter. Feel the

effect this has on you, and allow yourself to go with
this feeling.

- Step 4: Now see the beauty of the world outside, the light and
the energy. The scene is drawing you out; you are longing to
experience what is beyond your window.

- Step 5: Feel the energy from the sun rushing into your body
and lifting you up with the breeze. Feel your whole being
drawn to leave, to reach the world outside. Picture in your
mind a person or place you have not seen, or been to, for
some time.

- Step 6: This approach may result in the vibrational state, or
you could simply find yourself lifted up out of your body. You
may also find yourself in another location altogether.

Object Technique

- Step 1: Select an object that has a lot of importance to you
and place it somewhere in your home, as far as possible from
where you sleep. It could be something personal, like a piece of
jewelry, or even a framed photograph.

- Step 2: Now take a few steps back from the object and look
at it intently. Observe every detail of the object and note how
you feel.

- Step 3: Trace your steps back to the usual location of the
object. Observe how you feel as you do this and take in as
much as you can about the route you walk.

- Step 4: Now look intently at the usual location of the object
and again note how you feel.

- Step 5: Return to the current location of the object and try
to pay as much attention as possible to the route you walk.
Repeat the process from step 2 to step 5 several times.

- Step 6: Go through your usual relaxation and vibrational state techniques. When you feel ready, focus on lifting out of your physical body and reaching the object.

Lucid Dreaming Technique

Good for: Type 2 (sleeping/dream) people

- Step 1: Each night before going to sleep, remind yourself that, should you become conscious in your dream, you will have the opportunity to leave your body. Really believe this and try to build an emotional connection to the idea. Also go over the next steps so that you can recall them during your dream.

- Step 2: Once you are aware that you are dreaming, say out loud in the dream, "I am conscious that I am dreaming and I wish to have an out-of-body experience." For most people, the act of saying this out loud in the dream will be enough and you will probably find that you are propelled out of your body.

If you find that you do not have an OBE using this approach, you may still have some apprehension about leaving your body. Try re-reading Chapter 5, "Transforming Beliefs." It may also mean that you need to reach a deeper level of sleep. Use a relaxation technique before going to sleep, continue practicing this method, and bring in other techniques based on your profile.

Techniques for Visual People

Cloud Technique

Although probably the simplest technique I'm aware of, this has a special place in my heart since it was one that I used often when I was learning to induce OBEs for the first time. It is a very gentle method and is especially good for people who find very complex visualisations difficult.

The idea is to allow yourself to slowly shift from one state of awareness to another. The key is not to get too focused on the peaceful feelings and relaxing visuals, but to try to sense yourself in another location and really shift from one location (in your body) to another (out of your body), rather than just imagining it.

- Step 1: Use one of the relaxation techniques until you feel calm but alert. Imagine your body beginning to dissolve.

- Step 2: Feel that you are no longer in your room, or on the bed, or wherever you are physically. Feel yourself floating, and imagine that you are lying on a bed of clouds.

- Step 3: See clouds and sky all around you. Feel the wind on your body and the sun on your skin. Let yourself gently drift through the air and over landscapes.

- Step 4: Intensify this awareness of the the sky and clouds until you reach a peak and find yourself out of your body, or you experience exiting your body. (My first induced OBE used this method; I experienced a jolt, almost like electricity, and found myself floating above my body.)

Body of Light Technique

This technique was popularised by many esoteric writers at the turn of the twentieth century and has been used effectively for well over a hundred years. When coupled with some of my other techniques, such as immersion or the G-Technique, it can be extremely effective.

- Step 1: Lie in bed or relax in a comfortable recliner, close your eyes, and go through your relaxation technique.

- Step 2: Now begin to imagine a figure standing at the foot of your bed or floating above you. Try to see the details of this figure (it should look like you from behind.)

- Step 3: Now focus on the figure and start to see it shining and glistening with light. Try to intensify this to the point that it resembles the vibrational state.

- Step 4: Use a technique such as the Bellow's Breath to intensify this vibrational awareness.

- Step 5: Now try to shift your awareness to the point of view of the figure. Try to see and sense as if you were the figure until it becomes so real you realise that you have left your body or you experience the seperation process.

Self-Image Technique

Good for: Type 2 (sleeping/dream) people

This method is based on the idea of reaching your unconscious mind during the process of going to sleep, or shortly before.

- Step 1: Securely affix a large mirror to the ceiling above your bed. Alternately, you can draw the outline of your body on a large sheet of paper, or on a bed sheet, and affix that to the ceiling, or use a photograph of yourself.

- Step 2: Shortly before you would normally go to bed, lie down on top of the covers and look at the reflection or image of yourself above. If you are using a mirror, make gestures and movements with your face as if you are looking around the room from above. Spend about fifteen minutes focusing on your image.

- Step 3: Now get into bed and close your eyes, but try to hold the image of yourself in your mind as you go to sleep. You may find that this technique and the Audio/Visual Immersive Approach work well together.

- Step 4: Allow yourself to drift into sleep but, as with the Conscious Sleep Technique, try to hold the image of yourself as long as possible, and be aware of yourself falling asleep.

- Step 5: If you intensify this image and process each night, it can lead to an OBE. It can be coupled with the Sleep Interruption Method and an affirmation such as, "I will have a fully conscious out-of-body experience tonight."

Techniques for Auditory People

Infra-Liminal and Frequency

Good for: Type 2 (sleeping/dream) people

Frequencies have been shown by the Monroe Institute and others to be another tool for influencing our brain state, and thus aiding us in having OBEs. I have worked with subliminal hypnotic techniques and frequencies to induce the vibrational state as well as full OBEs. (I call this infra-liminal technology. See my website for more information.)

- Step 1: Using an Infra-liminal track or pink noise, focus your awareness on the sound and begin to sense your awareness expanding outward.

- Step 2: After approximately fifteen to twenty minutes, you will experience a change in your awareness. Colours and sensations may arise.

- Step 3: At this point, try to become aware of any sense of being at another location or a sense of the vibrational state beginning.

- Step 4: At this point you may exit the body naturally. If not, try combining this with the Object Technique.

Chanting Technique

- Step 1: Start by standing next to your bed or wherever you usually do your OBE exercises. Start to produce a simple hum. Imagine the sound of an electrical current or deep buzzing energy coming from within your body.

- Step 2: Breathe in and out with this buzzing energy. As each breath ends, try to increase the sense of vibration rushing through your body. Imagine that you are alive with the vibration of the sound.

- Step 3: As the sound reaches its peak, lie back on your bed or wherever you practice. Tense and relax your muscles as you let your full voice out.

- Step 4: Now start to draw the sound in. Focus less on the actual level of sound and more on the feeling of vibration inside you. Try to condense that feeling into your body until you can feel it without making any sound at all.

- Step 5: Now let that vibration move beyond the boundary of your body and go with the sensations. Allow yourself to lift up out of your body. Your legs and arms can lift out first, if that is easier.

Sleep Deprivation with Affirmations Technique

Good for: Type 2 (sleeping/dream) people

Breaking your normal sleep patterns can be a very powerful technique when coupled with affirmations. I have used this approach on retreats for nearly twenty years with a high level of success. Over the course of a week, set your alarm to wake you up during the night. The first time I tried this approach, I got up every day at dawn and recited a set of affirmations as the sky lightened.

Affirmations are an easy but powerful way to transmit a message to the unconscious mind. They consist of simply repeating a short statement to yourself, over and over. Another approach is to record the affirmation and play it back on loop at a low level as you relax. It is easy to make a recording of this type; all you need is a simple tape recorder or a computer with a built-in microphone. An example affirmation might be, "I will have a fully conscious out-of-body experience tonight and will have complete recollection of the entire experience."

Let's break this down into steps:

- Step 1: Set your alarm clock for thirty minutes before dawn (the exact times of sunrise and sunset can be found online at www.timeanddate.com)

- Step 2: Go to sleep as normal, but get up when your alarm goes off.

- Step 3: If you have a garden or other outdoor space, go there so that you may do your affirmations as the sun rises.

- Step 4: Sit in a comfortable, cross-legged posture on the ground or meditation cushion. Still your mind and relax as if you were going to meditate.

- Step 5: Begin to repeat the affirmation, "I will have a fully conscious out-of-body experience when I return to sleep and will have complete recollection of the entire experience." Alternatively, you can focus on being conscious in your dream (easier for many people) and then project from your lucid dream state. This is the method I have found most effective, personally. In this case, use the affirmation, "I will be fully conscious in my dream when I return to sleep."

- Step 6: After thirty minutes, return to bed and go back to sleep (an eye mask may help with this). After a few days of this you will likely have a fully conscious OBE upon returning to sleep.

Techniques for Physical People

G-Technique

The G-Technique is a method of breathing combined with muscle tension. I have found it very effective in revitalising the mind and exhausting the body. The "G" in the name refers to the G-force training that pilots undergo when they are learning to deal with the effects of gravity at high speeds. The technique they learn is designed to push all of the blood up into the brain to avoid them passing out under these conditions. Obviously our needs are not so extreme, but our variations on this technique result in muscle exhaustion and a heightened, almost nonphysical sensation. It can also lead to the vibrational state or even to a direct OBE in some cases. In fact, I experienced my most powerful OBE as a result of this technique. However, it's important to mention that if you suffer from any kind of blood pressure issues or heart conditions, please consult a doctor before attempting this approach.

There are two variations that differ mainly in the method of breathing used. Once you become more familiar with the process, you will find you can do it longer with the second version.

Version 1

- Step 1: Stand with your arms by your sides and your feet shoulder-width apart.

- Step 2: Slowly tense all of your muscles in an upward motion, from your toes to the top of your head. At the same time, draw in your breath.

- Step 3: Maintaining the tension, hold your breath for a count of three, and release.

- Step 4: Repeat the process until you feel energised. If you find that you feel dizzy or uncomfortable, stop and try one of the less strenuous techniques.

- Step 5: After performing the complete process three times, lie down and focus on the sensations you feel. You may experience the vibrational state—if so, use this state to exit the body by intensifying it and focusing your attention on a target but do not strain or push yourself.

Version 2

- Step 1: Stand with your arms by your sides and your feet shoulder-width apart.

- Step 2: Slowly tense all of your muscles in an upward motion, from your toes to the top of your head. At the same time, breathe in and then out on a count of one, two.

- Step 3: Continue for thirty seconds and stop. If you do not feel dizzy, uncomfortable, or exhausted, repeat the process until you reach a highly energised state. It can be hard to maintain the tension while breathing in and out. The focus should be on the outward breath, so if you have trouble doing both, just do the outward breath for a few moments and stop, rest, and then try again.

- Step 4: After performing the complete process three times, lie down and focus on the sensations you feel. You may experience the vibrational state—if so, use this state to exit the body by intensifying it and focusing your attention on a target but do not strain or push yourself.

The Bellows Breath (Bhastrika)

The Bellows Breath (Bhastrika) technique was one of the first approaches I learnt that uses the breath. I learnt it from Dr. Douglas Baker, my first mentor as a young teenager. He regularly gave lectures around London on Techniques of Astral Projection and the Bellows Breath. The idea is that, when you are on the brink of exiting the body, you can use the technique to tip the balance and essentially push yourself out. It is not seen as a method you would use on a regular basis, but at times when you are very close and need something extra.

The method actually originates in the yogic system of pranayama. There are of course variations and more advanced versions. If you want to explore those, I recommend finding a certified instructor who can you guide through the subtleties of the process in a safe way.

- Step 1: Kneel with your hands held in loose fists in front of you, your elbows by your ribcage.

- Step 2: Breathe in as forcefully as possible while pushing your arms up above your head and straightening your elbows and opening your hands widely.

- Step 3: Once your lungs are full, bring your arms down, exhaling forcefully until your elbows make contact with your ribcage and your lungs are fully empty. You may wish to make a hissing sound as you exhale, as this sometimes improves the ability to exhale fully.

- Step 4: Repeat this for twenty cycles, and then rest with your hands on your lap, opened upward, for thirty seconds to two minutes before repeating.

- Step 5: When applying this technique to the out-of-body state, you should already be at the point of leaving the body, maybe with heightened energy such as in the vibrational state, or with the sensation that parts of your body, such as your legs or arms, are floating out. This is when you can use the Bellows Breath effectively.

- Step 6: Now take a few deep breaths and focus your attention on what you are doing. Hold your breath for a few seconds before taking one breath, as fast and as sharply as you can, up through your nose. Repeat this if necessary in an even and consistent way while also maintaining the intensity of the in-breath. This should cause you to lift easily out of your body.

Focused Massage Technique

G. M. Glaskin first wrote about the idea of using some form of massage to aid in inducing out-of-body experiences. If you are working with a partner, I highly recommend this technique for two reasons. First, massage aids in relaxing the body and mind to the level required to have an OBE, and second, massage focused on the head and key areas of the body, such as the solar plexus, can help to bring on the vibrational state.

- Step 1: Starting at the side of the head, just above the ears, rotate your fingers in a circular motion. Continue this until you sense that your partner has relaxed and is allowing the weight of his or her head to rest in your hands.

- Step 2: Try lifting their head slightly and moving it from side to side very gently to get a sense of whether they are fully relaxed.

- Step 3: Now focus on the eyes, very gently applying a small amount of pressure to the closed eyelids, again rotating your fingers. As you do this, your partner should begin to focus out into the space ahead of him or her.

- Step 4: Now hold your index finger over your partner's third eye area—just above and between the eyebrows. Move your finger back and forth for a few minutes until your partner feels a strong tingling sensation.

- Step 5: Now, with your thumbs on your partner's temples and your index fingers on the third eye area, begin to make firm rotating motions. Keep this going for several minutes as your partner continues to focus his or her attention at a point out ahead. As the strong tingling sensation increases, they should move this point farther out. They might also use a visualisation technique or other approach alongside the massage.

- Step 6: As the person being massaged focuses further and further out, coupled with the sensations in their body, an OBE may follow.

Exhaustion Technique

Exhaustion is a very common tool for leaving the body; it can lead to an out-of-body experience with nothing else added. Usually all that is needed is a mental target such as in the Object Technique (see page 194) or an auditory approach, such as my Infra-liminal technology or a visual method like the Body of Light Technique.

- Step 1: Select a sport or activity that you enjoy and engage in it for long periods. Activities that I've found work for this technique include hiking, running, dancing, or yoga. Simply lacking in sleep will work as well.

- Step 2: Set aside a whole day or even several days to do your chosen activity. You must allow enough time to push yourself to a level of exhaustion that you would not normally reach.

- Step 3: As you do your activity, keep in mind your goal of leaving the body and try not to get mentally involved in what you are doing. The goal is physical, not mental, exhaustion.

- Step 4: Once you have completed a day of activity, lie down on your bed and take note of how you feel. You should feel like your body is totally ready to rest, but that your mind is still alert from the day's activity. At this point, use one of the other techniques suggested above in conjunction with this state and turn your focus towards leaving the body.

Techniques for Working with a Partner

Working with a partner is a great way of supporting the process of learning to have an OBE. There is no reason that you need to do so in isolation; in fact, I think support in most areas of life leads to a greater likelihood of success. But there are also other benefits to working with a partner: they can take an active role in helping you to achieve your goals, they can monitor you while you go through relaxation techniques, they can act as a guide in a meditation, and they even take care of a chore you would usually do to free up some time if you lead a busy lifestyle. They can also encourage you to stick to regular practice, which otherwise can become difficult. Working with an intimate partner or someone you feel comfortable with physically has the further benefit of making massage possible.

Meditation in which you focus on each other is useful in developing better focus and relaxation. But always do this at a separate time of day from your OBE practice; I have found that the more inward focus of meditation is not always helpful for leaving the body.

You may also want to try working in a group, although I would recommend keeping it small. I've found that a group of more than five people tends to become impersonal and stops being effective as a supportive aid.

The group structure will allow you to discuss your progress and get feedback from others. You might also consider retreats such as the ones I run, which allow you to fully immerse yourself in the best techniques over a weekend or longer. See my website, www.grahamnicholls.com, for more on retreats.

Emotional Link Technique

Good for: Type 2 (sleeping/dream) people

This simple technique is very effective for emotional people, and for those who work best with someone else. The idea is that you arrange with another person to attempt to learn to have OBEs together, at the same time at different locations. If you can't find someone to work with in this way, then a person that you haven't seen for some time, but would like to see, can be an alternative target. You simply try to project yourself to that person on a regular basis.

- Step 1: Before going to sleep, take an image of your partner or the person you want to reach, and focus on it. You may also want to do this constantly throughout the day. If you are using other techniques, such as the Audio/Visual Immersive Approach, you may want to have the image near as a reference to where you will travel once out of the body.

- Step 2: As you lie in bed, imagine the person and say their name out loud. You may even want to call out to them. Concentrate on your feelings about this person; reach out to them with your emotions.

- Step 3: Hold them in your mind as you go to sleep and try to imagine yourself being with them.

Sticky Hands Technique

Good for: Physical people

This approach is drawn from martial arts, where you learn how to react to subtle cues from another person. It helps with gaining a deeper understanding of and connection with a partner.

- Step 1: Stand facing your partner for a few minutes. Try to connect with them so that you feel you know what they are about to do.

- Step 2: Start to move slowly, in sync with each other. You may want to do this holding hands, but better still would be to do the exercise touching but not actually holding each other.

- Step 3: As you move, try to draw your partner into your movements so that you are "leading."

- Step 4: Now switch and allow the other person to lead. You will feel a natural point at which the dynamic switches to them. Just go with this and try to act as one unit as much as possible.

Visual Connection Technique

Good for: Visual people

- Step 1: Sit in a comfortable posture with your partner, either in chairs or on the floor. Make sure that the lighting is low and the temperature in the room is warm and comfortable, but not so warm as to make you sleepy.

- Step 2: Focus on each other's faces. Do not think about anything in particular; just try to sense their emotional state and the aspects of their personality that link you.

- Step 3: Try to sense what they are sensing about you. Imagine yourself in their position looking back at you. Try to feel what they feel and create a deeper bond between you.

- Step 4: Maintaining this awareness of the other person, lie down at opposite sides of the room or move to separate rooms.

- Step 5: Now try to sense the closeness of the other person again. Be with them in your mind until you begin to feel their presence beyond your imagination.

Technique for Accessing the Transphysical Levels

The transphysical (afterlife) levels are not easy to reach with any certainty. They are the furthest from our default awareness, and therefore require the greatest shift of understanding in order to reach them with full awareness. In my experience, this is best achieved through preparation over an extended period of time, during which a focus on someone who has passed over can be developed. I should also mention that this approach is for those who have already had some success with more general OBE techniques and feel that they will benefit from taking things to the next level. For this reason, it is assumed that you are able to bring on the vibrational state, and if not, that you are able to leave your body without it.

Below is a week-long plan for building up the necessary focus through purification and constant mental work. The approach gets more intensive as the week passes, so I recommend only starting when you know you will have time to see the whole process through.

As mentioned in Chapter 11, you should build up your energy to the point of exiting, but hold off to the last moment and then allow yourself to go as far as possible until you naturally reach your limit. If you have been focusing on the target person deeply enough, you will find that you are drawn to him or her.

Day 1

Morning
15–20 minutes of meditation
Breakfast: Fruit or smoothie

Daytime
Affirmations stating your goal of reaching the afterlife
    plane and contacting your target person
Lunch: Light vegan or raw meal
G-Technique

Evening
Dinner: Vegan dinner (no alcohol)
20 minutes of Ganzfeld or Three-Dimensional
  Doorway Technique

Day 2
Morning
15–20 minutes of meditation
Breakfast: Fruit or smoothie

Daytime
Affirmations
Lunch: Light vegan or raw meal

Evening
Dinner: Vegan dinner (no alcohol)
20 minutes Ganzfeld or Three-Dimensional
  Doorway Technique

Day 3
Morning
20–30 minutes of meditation
Breakfast: Fruit or smoothie

Daytime
Affirmations
Lunch: Light vegan or raw meal

Evening
Dinner: Vegan dinner (no alcohol)
5 minutes G-Technique (lie down after and
  focus on energies)

Day 4

Morning
20–30 minutes of meditation
Breakfast: Fruit or smoothie

Daytime
Affirmations
Lunch: Light vegan or raw meal

Evening
Dinner: Vegan dinner (no alcohol)
30 minutes Ganzfeld and 15 minutes
    Three-Dimensional Doorway Technique

Day 5

Morning
20–30 minutes of meditation
Breakfast: Fruit or smoothie

Daytime
Affirmations
Lunch: Light vegan or raw meal

Evening
Dinner: Vegan dinner (no alcohol)
5 minutes G-Technique (lie down after
    and focus on energies)

Day 6

Morning
20–30 minutes of meditation
Breakfast: Fruit or smoothie

Daytime

Affirmations

Lunch: Light vegan or raw meal

Evening

Dinner: Vegan dinner (no alcohol)

30 minutes Ganzfeld and 15 minutes

      Three-Dimensional Doorway Technique

Day 7

Morning

20–30 minutes of meditation

Breakfast: Fruit or smoothie

Daytime

Affirmations

Lunch: Light vegan or raw meal

Evening

Dinner: Vegan dinner (no alcohol)

5 minutes G-Technique (lie down after

    and focus on energies)

Note: As mentioned earlier, this is not a method for achieving an OBE; it is merely for preparing your body/mind for the process of reaching the transphysical levels. This programme can also be combined with the Sleep Deprivation and Affirmation Techniques, as reaching these levels may be easier when in deeper states between wakefulness and unconsciousness.

Glossary

Akasha: In Eastern religions and philosophies, akasha is the underlying essence of life, or the element believed to bind earth, air, fire, and water together. It is also often translated as spirit or aether. (See also *Akashic Record.*)

Akashic Record: In esoteric tradition, the akashic record is usually considered to be a component of the astral plane that contains the imprint of all events, knowledge, and thought throughout all of time. Practitioners of astral projection claim that this record can be accessed and insights into the past can be gained through it.

Astral Projection: In New Age, esoteric, and occult circles, astral projection is used to refer to the process of leaving the body in the form of an astral or subtle body, which believers see as one of many distinct bodies existing within, or closely around, the physical body. The definition of astral projection also often includes the more dreamlike states closely related to lucid dreaming, while the out-of-body experience is usually more specifically the state of full separation from the physical body in some form. (See also *Out-of-Body Experience.*)

Astral Body: In esoteric tradition, the astral body is usually considered the second of the subtle bodies after the etheric body or double. The astral body is considered to be emotional in nature and to inhabit the astral planes, an environment beyond the physical world that is far more malleable and more influenced by thought than everyday reality.

Binaural Beats: (See *Hemi-Sync®.*)

Crowley, Aleister: Born Edward Alexander Crowley in England in 1875 to a Plymouth Brethren family, Crowley had deep-rooted issues from the beginning with his extreme religious upbringing. As a result, he adopted a complex form of occultism, which later developed into his own version of the work of the Hermetic Order of the Golden Dawn, called Thelema (Greek for "will"). This new version drew on many diverse influences, from yoga to science to the use of sexuality as a magical tool. Due to his formidable intellect and radical ideas, Crowley remains highly influential in many areas, including astral projection. (See also *Hermetic Order of the Golden Dawn.*)

Extrasensory Perception: Extrasensory perception (ESP) is a general term, thought to have been coined by the British explorer Sir Richard Burton in 1870. It refers to psychic abilities such as telepathy and clairvoyance.

Etheric Body: Usually seen as the first of the subtle bodies, closely related to the Earth plane of existence. Like the astral body, the etheric double is commonly referred to in esoteric and occult literature, especially Theosophy and related traditions. But while the astral body moves around the astral planes, the etheric body moves within everyday reality.

Fenwick, Peter: Dr. Peter Fenwick is a British consultant neuro-psychiatrist at Maudsley Hospital, London. He has published more than two hundred papers in medical and scientific journals on brain function, including several papers on meditation and altered states of consciousness. He is widely regarded as the leading clinical authority in the U.K. on the subject of near-death experiences.

Ganzfeld: The term *Ganzfeld* comes from German and means "total or complete field," as in a field of sound or energy. The Ganzfeld technique is a mild form of sensory deprivation (sometimes called perceptual deprivation). It was developed in psychology, but has been widely used for many years within parapsychology as a way to induce a mild altered state, generally in members of the public volunteering for telepathy experiments.

Golden Dawn, The: (See *Hermetic Order of the Golden Dawn.*)

Hemi-Sync®: Developed by Robert A. Monroe and a group of scientists based on a brain effect discovered by Heinrich Wilhelm Dove in the nineteenth century called binaural beats. Hemi-Sync® is short for "hemispheric synchronization," an innovative technology that uses slightly distinct sound frequencies played through headphones. From the differential between the two sound sources, a further frequency, or binaural beat, is created. This in turn is thought to alter the brainwave state, allowing for a range of experiences including out-of-body experiences.

Hermetic Order of the Golden Dawn, The: An occult order with heavy Masonic influences, based in England during the late nineteenth and early twentieth centuries. The order was progressive for its time in that it admitted women, and has been extremely influential on modern occult and New Age thought, mainly due to the writings of Israel Regardie and Aleister Crowley. Other important members included the Irish poet W. B. Yeats, and Allan Bennett, who established the first Buddhist organisation in Britain.

Immersion: A term often used to refer to systems designed to affect all of our sensory awareness in some way, such as virtual reality or sensory deprivation, which involve either giving our senses imagery generated by a computer or simply removing our normal reliance on our senses. These approaches can allow us to experience an impossible world, in the case of virtual reality, or allow us to focus on our inner processes and inner dialogue in sensory deprivation. My own works (Epicene, 1998; LAM, 2001; and The Living Image, 2004) all use forms of sensory immersion to allow people to experience their conscious awareness in new ways.

Institute of Noetic Sciences, The: The Institute of Noetic Sciences (IONS) was founded in 1973 by Apollo 14 astronaut Edgar Mitchell. It is a nonprofit research, education, and membership organisation based in Petaluma, California. IONS conducts, sponsors, and collaborates on leading-edge research into psi and other areas related to extended consciousness.

Lucid Dream: A dream involving a heightened degree of consciousness, often characterised by the dreamer being able to control the course of the dream. Many writers on out-of-body experiences see lucid dreams as a useful way of launching into the out-of-body state. Some authors claim there is little or no difference between the two states. (Please refer to the section on dream and out-of-body experiences in Chapter 2 for more on this subject.)

McMoneagle, Joseph: Joseph McMoneagle was one of the key remote viewers in the U.S. military program that ran for twenty years, often referred to as Stargate. In 1984, he received the Legion of Merit award for determining 150 essential pieces of information about locations, mainly in the Soviet Union, via psychic means. He continues to undertake private remote viewing work and has helped locate many missing persons using the same methods. (See also *Remote Viewing*.)

Mindfulness: Is a concept generally associated with the various Buddhist teachings. It is considered one of the signs of enlightenment. In the context of this book, it means a heightened awareness of the reality of things, not distorted by emotional ups and downs.

Monroe, Robert A.: Robert A. Monroe (1915–1995) was an American businessman who in the later part of his life began having out-of-body experiences as a result of experimenting with sound frequencies. He was initially seeking ways to improve our ability to learn while we sleep, but instead found that he had an out-of-body experience. With a group of volunteer scientists, he later went on to develop Hemi-Sync® technology and founded the Monroe Institute. He was also the author of three books: *Journeys Out of the Body* (1971), *Far Journeys* (1985), and *Ultimate Journey* (1994).

Monroe Institute, The: The Monroe Institute was founded by Robert A. Monroe in the 1970s in Charlottesville, Virginia. The institute is a non-profit organisation focused on research into areas such as consciousness, education on related topics, and the use of Hemi-Sync®.

Near-Death Experience (NDE): An NDE is believed to take place when normal heart rate and brain activity has stopped, a condition which without medical intervention would lead to death. The outward signs of life are absent, yet the state is defined as "near death," since normal heart and brain function can still be recovered. While individuals are in this state, they appear to experience a form of independent consciousness that can observe events around the area of the physical body, or a range of other phenomena. A near-death experience appears to suggest an independent consciousness or spirit that can travel to nonphysical levels of reality. In many cases, the person will "see" a dark tunnel with a light at the end, where sometimes they will be greeted by their dead relatives. NDEs often include an all-pervading white light, characterised by a feeling of unconditional love and compassion. There have been many collections of accounts and studies on the subject, the most notable being by Pim Van Lommel, Peter Fenwick, Penny Sartori, and Jeffery Long.

Out-of-Body Experience (OBE or OOBE): An out-of-body experience is characterised by sensory awareness of total separation from one's physical body, in the form of a "double" or independent consciousness, whilst usually still being able to see and reason. The experience often involves perceiving the body from above, travel over distances, and sometimes interaction with others. The OBE can also lead to what appear to be other levels of reality, and is generally described as "being as real as everyday reality."

Parapsychology: A scientific discipline that began in a formal sense with the founding of the Society for Psychical Research in London in 1882. The field is focused on the use of the scientific method for the study of anomalous phenomena and questions related to the survival of consciousness after death. After 130 years of exploration, the field of parapsychology still faces much prejudice and little funding, but despite this has established evidence, at least as consistent as in other fields, showing that psychic abilities, such as telepathy or precognition, are scientifically demonstrable. (See also *Society for Psychical Research*.)

Placebo effect: The placebo effect is a measurable change in the health or wellbeing of a patient who is receiving some form of treatment that cannot be attributed to the treatment itself. In medical tests, it is common to give some of the participants a dummy pill such as a sugar pill and others the real medicine. Many of the people receiving the dummy pill will report improvements consistent with what they believe the pill was for.

Presence: Presence as a spiritual concept has become popular in recent years through the work of Eckhart Tolle. I would define it as a state of awareness of the present moment, which frees us from our emotions and beliefs about the past and future. If we see just what is, there is no emotional conflict deriving from what happened before, or what we imagine might happen in the future, The result is we are simply clear and aware. (See also *Mindfulness*.)

Psi: Psi is sometimes incorrectly pronounced as the separate initials, P S I, but is actually not an abbreviation; it is the twenty-third letter of the Greek alphabet, a symbol also used for more mainstream forms of psychology. It is seen as a neutral or scientific term for anomalous psychology, which would include things like psychic abilities and out-of-body experiences, but without any esoteric or supernatural associations. (See also *Parapsychology*.)

Psychic Research: (See *Parapsychology*.)

Precognition: The conscious awareness of a future event, usually through a mental image or dream state. Literally *pre*, as in "before" and *cognition*, as in "thought."

Presentiment: Similar to precognition in that presentiment is the sensing of a future event, yet presentiment is essentially the feeling rather than a thought or vision. Presentiment is also often more unconscious, especially when it is the focus in parapsychological testing, as in the work of Dean Radin, for example. Within these experiments, tiny changes in skin conductance, eye movement, or brain activity indicate an unconscious reaction to a shocking image that has yet to be shown. The subjects will be totally unaware of their reaction, yet by using advanced equipment, scientists such as Radin can monitor these reactions and demonstrate that some form of awareness of future events does occur.

Quantum Entanglement: In Quantum Physics, Entanglement refers to the separation of particles, such as photons (light particles) that were once connected, resulting in a state in which they continue to act as if they were one system or still entangled over any distance. This idea is interesting to this book because physicists such as Brian Josephson have put forward a theory (Biological Utilisation of Quantum Non-locality) that explores the possibility that Entanglement could be related to the function of psychic abilities in humans and other animals—essentially that brains, or consciousness itself, could be entangled and therefore experience elements of the perceptions of another person from a distance. This offers a scientific framework for how telepathy, to gave one example, could be possible.

Quantum Physics: Also called Quantum Mechanics or Quantum Theory, it is a form of science that began in approximately 1900, when Max Planck realised that atoms could only vibrate at limited, or quantised, frequencies. Quantum physics is an extremely complex and successful area of science dealing with indivisible units of energy called quanta that exist in the Quantum realm (the extremely small levels of reality). Quantum objects can exist in multiple states, and even at the same time. All of this makes this area extremely paradoxical and in many ways it contradicts the notion of an objective reality. For those interested to learn more on how this relates to the out-of-body state and the issues in this book, I would recommend the work of physicist and author of *My Big TOE (Theory Of Everything)*, Thomas Campbell.

Radin, Dean: Dean Radin is one of the leading U.S. researchers into psi and related areas. He is currently senior scientist at the Institute of Noetic Sciences (IONS) and adjunct faculty in the department of psychology at Sonoma State University. He is the author of two books, *Entangled Minds* and *The Conscious Universe*, which are widely considered the best introductions to parapsychology.

Remote Viewing: During the Cold War period, the U.S. military founded a secret program to investigate the use of psychic intelligence gathering. The program, known as *Project Stargate*, involved several phases and smaller sub-projects exploring different areas as ideas and methodologies developed. The project ran for twenty years and produced significant evidence for psychic functioning. Jessica Utts, who assessed the results of the project wrote, "It is clear to this author that anomalous cognition is possible and has been demonstrated. This conclusion is not based on belief, but rather on commonly accepted scientific criteria."[1] Several of the original members of the project are still active and have continued to offer evidence for psi, among them Ingo Swann and Joseph McMoneagle.

Sheldrake, Rupert: Dr. Rupert Sheldrake is a British biologist and psi researcher based in London. He is the author of more than eight scientific papers and ten books. He studied natural sciences at Cambridge University and philosophy at Harvard, and was also director of studies and a fellow of Clare College, Cambridge. He was the director of the Perrot-Warrick Project from 2005 to 2010, one of the few projects supporting parapsychological research.

Silver Cord: An object, somewhat like an umbilical cord made of energy, described by some as connecting the subtle body with the physical body. Although the concept of the silver cord has been around for a very long time—some even believing there are references to it in the Bible (Ecclesiastes 12:6)— it was likely Sylvan Muldoon and the book *Projection of the Astral Body* that popularized the notion. In recent years the presence of the cord in OBEs has become less commonly reported.

Sleep Paralysis: Sleep paralysis is the inability to move upon waking (although usually into a semi-dream state). The mind is active and aware, but the body will not respond normally. It can happen during the period of falling asleep (known as hypnogogic or predormital form) or when waking up (known as hypnopompic or postdormital form). Some elements of the experience seem to resemble the out-of-body state, although this has not been explored in enough detail to draw any conclusions.

Society for Psychical Research, The: The Society for Psychical Research was founded in 1882 in London, becoming the first organisation of its kind in the world. Still in existence today, it continues to undertake research and promote a scientific understanding of the nature of psychic abilities, and especially the question of survival of consciousness after death.

Swann, Ingo: Ingo Swann is an artist and author, but is best known for co-creating the system of controlled clairvoyance known as remote viewing. He was one of the key psychics involved in the military remote viewing program in the United States, which ran during the Cold War period. He has taken part in many scientific experiments into psi, and is widely considered a leading expert on the subject. (See also *Remote Viewing*.)

Tattva: Tattvas are a series of symbols originating in Indian religious philosophy, which represent the elements in nature—such as earth, air, fire, water, and aether or akasha—using simple shapes such as a circle or triangle. In Western occult interpretations, the tattvas are used as a method of entering into a trance state that can lead to a form of clairvoyant perception akin to a mild out-of-body experience.

Theosophical Society, The: Founded in 1875, the Theosophical Society is an international organisation promoting and educating in the aims and philosophy of Theosophy. (See also *Theosophy*.)

Theosophy: A philosophy or religious tradition that blends elements of Eastern and Western thought. Theosophy has been an influential source of much of contemporary New Age thought.

Transphysical: I use this term to describe the sensory awareness or level of consciousness after brain function has ceased. I use it as a more neutral term, like psi, to avoid making assumptions about an afterlife or the nature of the state we will experience after physical death. It indicates only that there appears to be some continuation of consciousness or awareness after brain activity has stopped.

Van Lommel, Pim: Pim Van Lommel was a cardiologist at the Rijnstate Hospital, Arnhem, in the Netherlands, from 1977 to 2003. During his time there, he conducted the most extensive research to date into the near-death experience. He continues to lecture and raise public awareness about the scientific understanding of the possible continuation of consciousness after death.

Vibrational State: The vibrational state is a sensation of energy experienced during the process of exiting the physical body. Although it is defined differently by both authors and the general public, some descriptions include a physical sensation arising from the core of the body, while others describe a strictly nonphysical vibration. Robert Bruce, author of *Astral Dynamics,* defines the vibrational state thus: "meaning strong, usually whole-body, energy-movement sensations, that are felt as vibrations in the physical body."[2] Yet Robert A. Monroe stated that the sensation or energy was nonphysical in nature.[137] My own experience suggests a wave sensation that has some physical elements, but is far more nonphysical. For example, it would not be visible to an onlooker, so may be best described as something between a physical sensation and a psychological shift.

Endnotes

Chapter 1

1. U.S. National Library of Medicine, "Hallucinations: Definition," MedlinePlus Database, http://www.nlm.nih.gov/medlineplus/ency/article/003258.htm.

2. Penny Sartori, *The Near-Death Experiences of Hospitalized Intensive Care Patients: A Five Year Clinical Study* (Lewiston, Queenston, Lampeter: The Edwin Mellen Press, 2008).

3. Ray Hyman, "Evaluation of a Program on Anomalous Mental Phenomena," *Journal of Scientific Exploration* 10, no. 1 (1996): 43.

Chapter 2

1. Rupert Sheldrake, "Consciousness and the Extended Mind," (Lecture Abstract, Royal College of Psychiatrists, Spirituality and Psychiatry Special Interest Group, 2009).

2. Rupert Sheldrake, "Answers to Your Most Frequently Asked Questions," http://www.sheldrake.org/Resources/faq/answers .html.

3. Rita Pizzi, Andrea Fantasia, Fabrizio Gelain, Danilo Rossetti, and Angelo Vescovi, "Quantum Information and Computation II." *Proceedings of the SPIE* (2004): 107–117.

4. Michael Persinger, interview with Alex Tsakiris, *Skeptiko* podcast 89, December 16, 2009.

5. Dean Radin, *Entangled Minds* (New York: Pocket Books, 2006), 120.

6. M. A. Persinger, "Propensity To Report Paranormal Experiences Is Correlated With Temporal Lobe Signs," *Perceptual and Motor Skills* 59 (1984): 583–586.

7. M. A. Persinger, "Geophysical Variables and Behavior: Intense Paranormal Experiences Occur During Days of Quiet Global Geomagnetic Activity," *Perceptual and Motor Skills* 61 (1985): 320-322.

8. Charles Tart, "Geomagnetic effects on GESP: Two studies," *Journal of the American Society of Psychical Research* 82 (1988), 193–216.

9. S. Krippner, A. Becker, M. Cavallo, and B. Washburn, "Electrophysiological Studies of ESP in Dreams: Lunar Cycle Differences in 80 Telepathy Sessions," *Human Dimensions* (1972), 14–19.

10. Ingo Swann, "The Emergence of Project SCANATE," *Remote Viewing—The Real Story!* (unpublished manuscript, 1995).

11. Pim Van Lommel, "About the Continuity of Our Consciousness, Brain Death and Disorders of Consciousness," *Advances in Experimental Medicine and Biology* 550 (2004), 115-132.

12. Pim Van Lommel, "Near-Death Experience, Consciousness, and the Brain: A New Concept About the Continuity of Our Consciousness Based on Recent Scientific Research on Near-Death Experience in Survivors of Cardiac Arrest," *World Futures* 62 (2006): 134–151.

13. BBC News Online, "Nurse Writes Book on Near-Death," http://news.bbc.co.uk/2/hi/uk_news/wales/7463606.stm. (June 19, 2008.)

Chapter 3

1. *Merriam-Webster's Collegiate Dictionary*, 11th ed., "Skepticism."

2. Carl Sagan, "Encyclopaedia Galactica," *Cosmos* 12: 01:24 minutes.

3. Marcello Truzzi, "Editorial," *The Zetetic* 1, no. 1 (Fall/Winter, 1976): 4.

4. Marcello Truzzi, *The Zetetic Scholar* 12-13 (1987).

5. Chris Carter, "Research of the Skeptics," Skeptical Investigations, http://www.skepticalinvestigations.org/Anomali/skeptic_research.html.

6. Susan Blackmore, *Journal of the American Society for Psychical Research* 83 (April 1989): 152.

7. Susan Blackmore, "An Evening with James Randi and Friends," lecture, Conway Hall, London. 2008.

8. Susan Blackmore, interview with Alex Tsakiris, *Skeptiko* podcast 114, Sept. 21, 2010.

9. Susan Blackmore, "OBEs and Sleep Paralysis" (paper for presentation at the 23rd International Conference of the Society for Psychical Research, Durham, United Kingdom 1999).

10. Ibid.

11. Andy Coghlan, "Out-of-body Experiences Are 'All in the Mind,'" *New Scientist*, http://www.newscientist.com/article/dn12531-outofbody-experiences-are-all-in-the-mind.html.

12. Dr. Peter Fenwick, interview with the author, March 31, 2011.

13. Andy Coghlan, "Out-of-Body Experiences Are 'All in the Mind,'" *New Scientist*, http://www.newscientist.com/article/dn12531-outofbody-experiences-are-all-in-the-mind.html.

14. Jan Holden, Jeff Long, and Jason MacLurg, "Out-of-Body Experiences: All in the Brain?", *International Association for Near-Death Studies*, http://www.iands.org/research/important-research-articles/69-out-of-body-experiences-all-in-the-brain.html?start=3.

15. James Randi, "Caltech Lecture Recording," James Randi Educational Foundation, 1992.

16. Randi's dishonest claims about dogs by Rupert Sheldrake (accessed January 2012) http://www.skepticalinvestigations.org/Mediaskeptics/Randi_dogs.html.

Chapter 5

1. Richard Bandler, *Time for a Change* (Cupertino, CA: Meta Publications, 1993).

Chapter 6

1. Dean Radin, *The Conscious Universe: The Scientific Truth of Psychic Phenomena* (New York: HarperOne, 1997).

Chapter 7

1. Milton R. Mills, M.D., "The Comparative Anatomy of Eating," http://www.vegsource.com/news/2009/11/the-comparative-anatomy-of-eating.html.

Chapter 8

1. V. C. Rubin, "Dark Matter in the Universe," *Scientific American Presents* 9, no. 1 (1998): 106–110.

2. Duncan MacDougall, "Hypothesis Concerning Soul Substance Together with Experimental Evidence of The Existence of Such Substance," *American Medicine* (April 1907).

3. Ibid.

4. Ibid.

5. Ibid.

6. The Global Consciousness Project, "An Introduction," http://gcp.grama.co/introduction-gcp.

Chapter 9

1. Robert Monroe, *Journeys Out of the Body* (Garden City, NY: Doubleday, 1971).

2. Aleister Crowley, *Magick: In Theory and Practice* (Secaucus, NJ: Castle Books, 1991).

Chapter 10

1. Dean Radin, "Entangled Minds Blog," http://deanradin.blogspot.com/2006/10/effects-of-distant-intention-on-water.html.

2. Dean Radin, "Entangled Minds Blog," http://deanradin.blogspot.com/2009/01/water-crystal-replication-study.html.

Chapter 11

1. Robert Monroe, interview on KPIX San Francisco, 1979. http://www.youtube.com/watch?v=4qcr7FfYloY.

2. Sylvan Muldoon and Hereward Carrington, *Projection of the Astral Body* (Whitefish, MT: Kessinger Publishing, 2003).

3. Dr. Peter Fenwick, interview with author, March 31, 2011.

Chapter 12

1. Dean Radin, "Electrodermal Presentiments of Future Emotions," *Journal of Scientific Exploration* 18, no. 2 (2004): 253–273.

Chapter 13

1. Samuel C. Eby, *The Story of the Swedenborg Manuscripts* (New York: New-Church Press, 1926).

2. C. W. Leadbeater, *A Textbook of Theosophy* (Charleston, SC: Forgotten Books, 2008).

Glossary

1. Jessica Utts, "An Assessment of the Evidence for Psychic Functioning" *Journal of Scientific Exploration* 10, no. 1 (1996) 3–30.

2. Robert Bruce, *Astral Dynamics: A New Approach to Out-of-Body Experience* (Charlottesville, VA: Hampton Roads, 1999).

3. Robert Monroe, interview on KPIX San Francisco, 1979. http://www.youtube.com/watch?v=4qcr7FfYloY.

Bibliography

Baker, Douglas. *The Opening of the Third Eye.* Wellingborough, UK: Aquarian Press, 1977.

———. *Practical Techniques of Astral Projection.* Wellingborough, UK: Aquarian Press, 1986.

Bandler, Richard. *Time for a Change.* Cupertino, CA: Meta Publications, 1993.

Bandler, Richard, and John Grinder. *The Structure of Magic: A Book about Language and Therapy.* Palo Alto, CA: Science and Behavior Books, 1975.

———. *Frogs into Princes: Neuro-linguistic Programming.* Moab, UT: Real People Press, 1979.

Blackmore, Susan J. *Beyond the Body: An Investigation of Out-of-the-Body Experiences, with a New Postscript by the Author.* Chicago: Academy Chicago Publishers, 1992.

———. *Dying to Live: Near-Death Experiences.* Buffalo, NY: Prometheus Books, 1993.

———. *In Search of the Light: The Adventures of a Parapsychologist.* Amherst, NY: Prometheus Books, 1996.

Brennan, J. H. *Astral Doorways.* London: Aquarian Press, 1971.

———. *Mindreach.* Wellingborough, UK: Aquarian Press, 1985.

———. *The Astral Projection Workbook: How to Achieve Out-of-Body Experiences.* New York: Sterling Pub. Co., 1989.

———. *Discover Astral Projection: How to Achieve Out-of-Body Experiences.* Rev. ed. London: Aquarian Press, 1991.

Bruce, Robert. *Astral Dynamics: A New Approach to Out-of-Body Experience.* Charlottesville, VA: Hampton Roads, 1999.

Bucke, Richard Maurice. *Cosmic Consciousness,* 20th ed. New York: Dutton, 1960.

Buhlman, William. *Adventures Beyond the Body: How to Experience Out-of-Body Travel.* San Francisco: HarperSanFrancisco, 1996.

———. *The Secret of the Soul: Using Out-of-Body Experiences to Understand Our True Nature.* San Francisco: HarperSanFrancisco, 2001.

Campbell, T. Colin, and Thomas M. Campbell. *The China Study: The Most Comprehensive Study of Nutrition Ever Conducted and the Startling Implications for Diet, Weight Loss and Long-term Health.* Dallas, TX: BenBella Books, 2005.

Campbell, Thomas. *My Big Toe.* Lightning Strike Books, 2003.

Cavendish, Richard, and J. B. Rhine. *Encyclopedia of the Unexplained: Magic, Occultism, and Parapsychology.* London: Arkana, 1989.

Clulee, Nicholas H. *John Dee's Natural Philosophy: Between Science and Religion.* London: Routledge, 1988.

Crowley, Aleister. *Magick: in Theory and Practice.* Secaucus, NJ: Castle Books, 1991.

Darwin, Charles, and Gillian Beer. *On the Origin of Species.* Rev. ed. New York: Oxford University Press, 2008.

Dee, John. *Private Diary of Dr. John Dee.* General Books, 2010.

Dick, Philip K. *The Minority Report.* New York: Pantheon Books, 2002.

Dunne, J. W. *An Experiment with Time.* New York: Macmillan Company, 1927.

Eby, Samuel C. *The Story of the Swedenborg Manuscripts.* New York: New-Church Press, 1926.

Einstein, Albert. Relativity, *The Special and the General Theory: A Popular Exposition by Albert Einstein.* New York: Crown Publishers, 1961.

Einstein, Albert, and S. W. Hawking. *Selections from the Principle of Relativity.* Philadelphia: Running Press, 2002.

Fenwick, Peter, and Elizabeth Fenwick. *The Truth in the Light: An Investigation of over 3000 Near-Death Experiences.* London: Headline, 1995.

———. *Past Lives: An Investigation into Reincarnation Memories.* New York: Berkley Books, 2001.

Fox, Oliver. *Astral Projection: A Record of Out-of-the-Body Experiences.* 6th ed. Secaucus, NJ: Citadel Press, 1980.

Green, Celia Elizabeth. *Out of the Body Experiences.* Institute of Psychophysical Research, 1973.

Head, Richard. *Mother Shipton's Prophecies: The Earliest Editions, with an Introduction*. Maidstone, UK: Mann, 1979.

Hyman, Ray. "Evaluation of a Program on Anomalous Mental Phenomena." *Journal of Scientific Exploration* 10, no. 1 (1996): 43.

Iyengar, B. K. S. *Light on Yoga: Yoga Dipika*. Rev. ed. New York: Schocken Books, 1979.

Iyengar, B. K. S., Yehudi Menuhin, and Ranganath Ramachandra Diwakar. *Light on Pranayama*. New York: Crossroad Publishing Company, 2004.

Jung, C. G., and R. F. C. Hull. *The Archetypes and the Collective Unconscious*. 2nd ed. Princeton, NJ: Princeton University Press, 1980.

Kapleau, Philip. *The Three Pillars of Zen: Teaching, Practice, and Enlightenment*. 25th anniv. ed. New York: Anchor Books, 1989.

Laureys, Steven, and Giulio Tononi. *The Neurology of Consciousness: Cognitive Neuroscience and Neuropathology*. Amsterdam: Elsevier Academic Press, 2009.

Lawson, Thomas T. *Carl Jung, Darwin of the Mind*. London: Karnac, 2008.

Lawton, Ian. *The Little Book of the Soul: Strange but True Stories that Could Change Your Life Forever*. Rational Spirituality Press, 2007.

Leadbeater, C. W. *The Chakras: A Monograph*. Wheaton, IL: Theosophical Pub. House, 1927.

———. *Astral Plane: Its Scenery, Inhabitants, and Phenomena*. Minneapolis, MN: Filiquarian Publishing, 2006.

———. *A Textbook of Theosophy*. Charleston, SC: Forgotten Books, 2008.

Long, Jeffrey, and Paul Perry. *Evidence of the Afterlife: The Science of Near-death Experiences*. New York: HarperOne, 2010.

McKnight, Rosalind A. *Cosmic Journeys: My Out-of-Body Explorations with Robert A. Monroe.* Charlottesville, VA: Hampton Roads, 1999.

McMoneagle, Joseph. *Mind Trek: Exploring Consciousness, Time, and Space through Remote Viewing.* Charlottesville, VA: Hampton Roads, 1993.

———. *The Ultimate Time Machine: A Remote Viewer's Perception of Time and Predictions for the New Millennium.* Charlottesville, VA: Hampton Roads, 1998.

Mitchell, Janet Lee. *Out-of-Body Experiences: A Handbook.* Jefferson, NC: McFarland, 1981.

Monroe, Robert A. *Journeys Out of the Body.* Garden City, NY: Doubleday, 1971.

———. *Ultimate Journey.* New York: Doubleday, 1996.

———. *Far Journeys.* New York: Broadway Books, 2001.

Muldoon, Sylvan Joseph, and Hereward Carrington. *The Projection of the Astral Body.* Alexandria, VA: Time-Life Books, 1990.

Nicholls, Graham. *Avenues of the Human Spirit.* Alresford, UK: O-Books, 2011.

Persinger, Michael A. *The Paranormal.* New York: MSS Information Corp., 1974.

———. *Neuropsychological Bases of God Beliefs.* Westport, CT: Praeger, 1987.

———. *ELF and VLF Electromagnetic Fields Effects.* New York: Plenum Press, 1974.

Peterson, Robert. *Out of Body Experiences: How to Have Them and What to Expect.* Charlottesville, VA: Hampton Roads, 1997.

Powell, A. E. *The Development of Astral Powers.* Whitefish, MT: Kessinger Publishing, 2010.

———. *The Etheric Double: The Health Aura.* Chennai, India: Theosophical Pub. House, 2000.

———. *The Astral Body and Other Astral Phenomena.* Wheaton, IL: Theosophical Publishing House, 1982.

Radin, Dean I. *The Conscious Universe: The Scientific Truth of Psychic Phenomena.* New York: HarperEdge, 1997.

———. *Entangled Minds: Extrasensory Experiences in a Quantum Reality.* New York: Paraview Pocket Books, 2006.

Randi, James. *The Mask of Nostradamus.* New York: Scribner, 1990.

Regardie, Israel, and Chris Monnastre. *The Golden Dawn: A Complete Course in Practical Ceremonial Magic.* 6th ed. St. Paul, MN: Llewellyn, 1998.

Richards, Steve. *The Traveller's Guide to the Astral Plane.* Wellingborough, UK: Aquarian Press, 1983.

Roberts, Henry C., Lee Roberts Amsterdam, and Harvey Amsterdam. *The Complete Prophecies of Nostradamus.* Rev. ed. Oyster Bay, NY: Nostradamus Co., 1982.

Russell, Ronald. *The Journey of Robert Monroe: From Out-of-Body Explorer to Consciousness Pioneer.* Charlottesville, VA: Hampton Roads, 2007.

Sagan, Carl. *The Demon-Haunted World: Science as a Candle in the Dark.* New York: Random House, 1996.

Sheldrake, Rupert. *New Science of Life.* New York: Putnam Publishing Group, 1983.

———. *The Sense of Being Stared At: And Other Aspects of the Extended Mind.* New York: Crown Publishers, 2003.

———. *Morphic Resonance: The Nature of Formative Causation.* 4th ed. Rochester, VT: Park Street Press, 2009.

————. *Dogs That Know When Their Owners Are Coming Home.* Rev. ed. New York: Three Rivers Press, 2011.

Stiene, Bronwen, and Frans Stiene. *The Reiki Sourcebook.* Alresford, UK: O-Books, 2008.

Tolle, Eckhart. *The Power of Now: A Guide to Spiritual Enlightenment.* Novato, CA: New World Library, 1999.

Van Lommel, Pim. *Consciousness Beyond Life: The Science of the Near-death Experience.* New York: HarperOne, 2010.

Wassermann, Gerhard D. *Shadow Matter and Psychic Phenomena: A Scientific Investigation into Psychic Phenomena and Possible Survival of the Human Personality after Bodily Death.* Oxford: Mandrake of Oxford, 1993.

Woolley, Benjamin. *The Queen's Conjurer: The Science and Magic of Dr. John Dee, Adviser to Queen Elizabeth I.* New York: Henry Holt, 2001.

Yram. *Practical Astral Projection.* Whitefish, MT: Kessinger Publishing, 2005.

Index